# FAULKNER:

## Fifty Years After
### *The Marble Faun*

EDITED BY

GEORGE H. WOLFE

THE UNIVERSITY OF ALABAMA PRESS
*University, Alabama*

THIRD PRINTING 1980

**Library of Congress Cataloging in Publication Data**

Main entry under title:

Faulkner, 50 years after The marble faun.
    Essays originally presented at a symposium held
at The University of Alabama, Oct. 1974
    Includes index.
    1. Faulkner, William, 1897–1962—Addresses,
essays, lectures.    I. Wolfe, George Hubert, 1942–
PS3511.A86Z7832114        813′5.2        75–40380
ISBN 0–8173–7609–7

# Contents

# *Preface*

The following essays were delivered originally as papers at a symposium held at The University of Alabama in October 1974. If the gathering was indeed the success that many kind people declared it to be, then most of the credit is due these scholars who participated with their writing, time, wit, and conversation.

The proceedings speak largely for themselves, I believe, requiring little by way of editorial introduction to justify or explain them. The purpose of the symposium was to bring together some of the best available Faulkner commentators and ask them to commemorate the 50th anniversary of the appearance of *The Marble Faun*, the author's first published volume. They have done so admirably.

It remains then to thank publicly the administration of The University of Alabama and the College of Arts and Sciences for their willing and unrestricted support of the original symposium and to state again my appreciation to numerous members of the Department of English, faculty, graduate students, and secretaries who contributed generously to its success. Also, special thanks go to the staff of The University of Alabama Press for their expert assistance on the book itself.

*University, Alabama*                       G.H.W.

# one   Joseph Blotner

# The Sole Owner
# and Proprietor

It was probably early 1936 when William Faulkner drew the map that formally staked out his claim as Sole Owner and Proprietor of Yoknapatawpha County. He had been mining that lode for nearly a decade by then, and he might have felt he was now tracing its boundaries as the first Jason Compson and Thomas Sutpen had marked theirs. Like the chronology that he had drawn up—first for himself and later for the readers of *Absalom, Absalom!*—it provided some help through the novel's complexities. He probably enjoyed doing the map more than the chronology, for he had shown his talent with brush and pen very early, and much of his art work was of professional caliber. But I suspect that the map may have unfolded and developed for him as some of his stories had done. When the *Viking Portable Faulkner* was published, he had told Malcolm Cowley in appreciation, "By God, I didn't know myself what I had tried to do, and how much I had succeeded."[1] I think that, as he drew the map, ten years before he wrote that letter, he must have had a similar sense of a whole domain spread out, a creation various and myriad like life itself. We know nothing of how he came into the ownership, how he had elaborated the county and its families in story after story and novel after novel. What sort of proprietor was he? What was his relationship as man and artist to this world he had created, which he would labor over for a full quarter century more?

It was not a constant relationship but one that changed with the years. It was always, of course, a vehicle for self-expression, for his total response to life. When he was young it provided an

1

outlet for anguish and aspiration, an opportunity to act out roles vicariously in a world of his own creation. When he was older, his writing provided an opportunity to express deeply felt views about contemporary life in particular and the human condition in general. By then, of course, it was not just a series of works that demanded some sort of disciplined form collectively just as they did individually. It was intensely personal, a way of leaving a mark, as he would put it, before passing through the wall of oblivion. He would say, with something like deprecation, that one of his editors regarded his work as an edifice, but I think that more and more he came to share that view, at least to see a large outline that he must fill in before he could—as he liked to put it—break the pencil and stop. Inevitably, the process became more self-conscious. How this fact affected the work itself forms still another question. Perhaps we can approach this subject by looking at a twin process: the way William Faulkner put himself into his work, and the way he regarded that body of work.

One thing that distinguishes him at the outset is his relationship to his craft. When one thinks of other American writers, one is aware of the other things they could do. One thinks of Twain as pilot and newspaperman, of Ernest Hemingway as foreign correspondent and contract magazine writer. A high school dropout, less well educated in the formal sense than many fellow artists, Faulkner sold stories and sketches to a New Orleans paper in his late twenties, but he was thirty-five before he had the chance to earn badly needed money through film-writing. All in all, he spent a total of about four years working at films, and this was his major distraction from his true metier, a necessary but costly one. He would talk, later on, about the demands that farming made on his time, but this was occasional work that he enjoyed and needed but not for financial reasons. All of this means, I think, that for almost all of his working life, his writing constituted a commitment paralleled in intensity and extent by that of very few other artists. Let us see what we can learn about this effort over the near half-century it spanned. Perhaps one generalization we can make is that it began as an intensely personal kind of writing despite its use of familiar forms, that with time it became more public, embracing concerns of the larger world outside, and that as the career drew to a close it moved toward the personal once more, but arriving as it did so at something of a synthesis between the two.

As a growing boy, Billy Falkner was as active as the next one. More than that, he led his brothers in games, hobbies, and deviltry. Keen-eyed, quick-minded, and active, he was a natural leader. In his middle teens he began to show signs of changing. He still played baseball and football, rode and hunted, but he fell in love, he found school increasingly boring, and he stopped growing. He became more the observer than the doer, more introspective than outgoing, and the power of imagination took over a larger and larger part of his life. His brother Jack passed him in height and his brother John in athletic ability. He had a high, somewhat thin voice, and in adolescence his boyish good looks had begun to desert him. As a mature man he would possess a striking face and head, but in his late teens, as he must have been measuring himself against the numerous other boys who clustered around the girl he loved, he must have known that he could not compete with many of them in physical appearance. As much as ten years later, he would look in the mirror and describe what he saw as "that ugly, ratty-looking face, that mixture of childishness and unreliability and sublime vanity. . . ."[2]

From childhood he had read avidly and written stories. No longer attending school, he read more and wrote more. He would later say, "I read and employed verse, firstly, for the purpose of furthering various philanderings in which I was engaged. . . . Later, my concupiscence waning, I turned inevitably to verse, finding therein an emotional counterpart far more satisfactory for two reasons: (1) No partner was required (2) It was so much simpler just to close a book, and take a walk. . . ."[3] I suspect strongly that these jaded remarks were as much a part of a pose as the kind of writing he had described. But often the work *was* personal. I think it is useful here to recall a line he gave one character in *Mosquitoes:* "you don't commit suicide when you are disappointed in love. You write a book."[4] He had written before he knew Estelle Oldham, and he would continue to write after he lost her, but that loss, and other unhappy love affairs, cannot but have intensified the process of turning to the inner world and especially to the increasingly absorbing process of creating art, of creating a world that he could order as he chose.

It may be instructive to look at some of this early work before we move on to Yoknapatawpha to see if we can find any places where the two worlds seem to cross. Much of the melancholy poetry of his late teens must simply have been his attempt at a traditional form of poetic plaint, even an imitation of specific poets such as Housman and Eliot. But in other verses he struck a note that sounded too personal to be imitation, as in the quatrain:

> It is vain to implore me
>    I have given my treasures of art
> Even though she choose to ignore me
>    And my heart.[5]

There was a carryover into his earliest publications, "L'Aprés-Midi d'un Faune" and *The Marble Faun*. Again one could argue that poets had been using fauns for centuries, but something about the static quality of Faulkner's fauns suggests a more personal significance. The protagonists of his first two novels would be described as having faunlike qualities, and a sketch that Faulkner later did, for the two children who would become his stepdaughter and stepson, showed lambs gamboling to tunes piped by a seated faunlike figure under a tree, and the figure he had drawn looked more like himself than it did like Pan. And his laments for lost love and fleeting beauty sounded like more than literary exercises.

Something of the same pattern of personal borrowing appeared in his early prose. Once in training, the first big achievement of the aviation cadet is solo flight. Nothing in the surviving official or newspaper accounts indicates that Faulkner's class had time for this before World War I ended. I think that through Cadet Thompson, in "Landing in Luck," Faulkner's first published short story, one can see clearly the vicarious achievement of that dream. Faulkner carried the process further with Cadet Julian Lowe in his first novel, *Soldiers' Pay*, but there the emphasis was not upon success but failure, that is, the failure to experience the ultimate: aerial combat in France. The despised white cap band that stigmatized the cadet, the admiration for those blooded, even maimed, in combat, these elements in the novel were consistent with what a young man like Faulkner, his imagination fed on such lore long before he reached Canada, must have felt. He had treated the figure of the maimed and doomed hero as early as his poem, "The Lilacs," which probably dates from about 1919. But by the time of *Soldiers' Pay* this figure had taken an even firmer hold upon his imagination; indeed, he had acted out the the part for unsuspecting friends in New Orleans and elsewhere. In his art he could give this figure shape and substance and pathos far exceeding anything he could achieve in personal masquerade, though that had been good enough to fool Sherwood Anderson, who had based just such a fictional character on Faulkner and called him "a little Southern man" named David, in a story called "A Meeting South." That name had appealed to Faulkner, and he had used it, in a story called "The Leg," for a young American who had lost a leg in France but gone on to aerial combat in spite of it. He had used the same name, in manuscript, for the protagonist of his strangest story, "Carcassonne," a plotless surrealist presentation of a possessed poet, his wild imagination ranging over heaven and earth.

In these early years Faulkner had still thought of himself as a poet. In a way he was like Joseph Conrad, regarding himself through the writing of his early novels as a sailor temporarily diverting himself with fiction until his next command turned up. But if Faulkner was moving further towards prose, he had abandoned none of the intensity he associated with poetry. Elements of both figures I have been discussing appeared in his second novel. The steward, David, in *Mosquitoes*, was the passive and suffering lover, utterly conquered by the Diana-like beauty that seems to have been Faulkner's ideal. The bearded sculptor, Gordon, looked something like Faulkner's friend, Bill Spratling, but his anguished devotion to his art linked him directly with the

David of "Carcassonne." The stream-of-consciousness of that David had been filled with images of agony and crucifixion. There were similar elements in that of Gordon, who thought not only of the wood he had been shaping but also of another creation: "By his own hand an autogethsemane carved darkly out of pure space. . . ."[6] Faulkner would write of having known "the agony of ink," of "the travail of invention and the drudgery of putting seventy-five or a hundred thousand words on paper. . . ."[7] One should not forget, of course, the kind of fertility of imagination, the inventive compulsion that was a part of his gift, that had made his cousin say, as early as childhood, "It got so that when Billy told you something, you never knew if it was the truth or just something he'd made up," that had made his uncle say, "He never was nothin, but a writer."[8] So again there was this pairing of elements, the irrepressible creative urge and the effort and strain that creation produced. Later he would often say that the writer was demon-driven, but that his demon would sometimes wake him in the morning with the enticement, "Come on, get up, try it, it's fun." This ambivalence got into the writing as it did the retrospective reflection, but he had accepted his vocation, his "doom," even though he felt at times that he was writing only for himself.

I should not leave *Mosquitoes* without noting one unique part of it. Though Faulkner would draw on his life extensively years later in the semi-autobiographical essay "Mississippi," *Mosquitoes* was the only published work in which he used himself explicitly. Jenny, the fleshy Venus of the voyage, described "A little kind of black man. . . . No. He was a white man, except he was awful sunburned and kind of shabby dressed—no necktie and hat. . . . He said he was a liar by profession, and he made good money at it, enough to own a Ford as soon as he got it paid out. I think he was crazy. Not dangerous: just crazy." With questioning she finally recalled his name: "I remember—Faulkner, that was it."[9] Faulkner's friend, Ben Wasson, recalled that the author was amused by this personal reference.

Nearly twenty years later, Faulkner would write Malcolm Cowley, "I am telling the same story over and over, which is myself and the world."[10] He told Phil Stone that he felt that people did what they could, but that by and large they were shaped by heredity. Something of both of these attitudes became more and more strongly imbued in the fiction from the time of *Flags in the Dust* onwards. Faulkner was tracing his family lines but at the same time picking up where he had left off in "Landing in Luck," by projecting upon his characters—here the flying Sartoris twins—not only the aspirations he had been unable to fulfill but also the kind of dark, adventurous, and fatal persona he sometimes desired. It was as though he were creating for himself the kind of mask, the kind of opposite that Yeats had in mind in many of his poems and in the poetic process by which, he said, "it is myself that I remake." Comparing Faulkner with his brothers, one can see why fiction would provide such an outlet. He was the smallest of the four. Jack was a rugged combat veteran, John was handsome and outgoing, and Dean was so versatile that Faulkner was later to tell Dean's daughter, "Your father was a rainbow."[11] Short, slight, and growing habitually more silent, Faulkner could fulfill himself in his fiction. The Sartoris twins went up in balloons and swung from water towers; without a parachute John leaped from his burning plane with jaunty gestures to his German foe and to his agonized brother; Bayard tried to expiate his guilt and kill his misery by horse and car, before succeeding spectacularly with an airplane.

Once again, to set up another pairing of opposites, Faulkner projected something of himself in the book that followed. He would say of *The Sound and the Fury* that it was a book he began to write for himself, without thought of publishers, an intensely private work in which he would create a little girl, a figure that moved him more than any other in all of his work. Each of the characters would be seen most significantly as they related to Caddy, and of these the most important is Quentin Compson. Nearly three decades later Faulkner would say to one friend, "Ishmael is the witness in Moby Dick as I am Quentin in *The Sound and the Fury*."[12] If he was speaking truly, what he had done in the character of Quentin was to employ for the purposes of his art his own concern over the past, especially the

Southern past, his unhappiness in love, and his compassion for the powerless and suffering, and he pushed these obsessive concerns to their logical resultant, just as the resultant of another complex of attitudes had produced the fatal vainglory of the Sartoris twins.

If he had found the rejection of *Flags in the Dust* traumatic, he found its reception, when it appeared in revised form as *Sartoris*, disappointing. "I think I not only won't ever make any money out of what I write," he told Stone, "I won't ever get any recognition either."[13] He might have begun *The Sound and the Fury* for himself alone, but it had turned into a publishable work, and just as the various poses he adopted consisted of cries for attention as well as protective masks, so he meant his work to gain him recognition. He might later say that, as a poet, he cared not for glory, but he wanted the recognition, the renown, all the same. He would gain a little more with each book, but it came slowly and it was not enough. Fitzgerald and Hemingway had gained theirs as young men. It would be years before Faulkner received anything like the general recognition they were accorded, and, when he finally did receive it in something like that measure, he would greet it almost with indifference and the accompanying publicity with outrage.

Three and a half months after *The Sound and the Fury* was published he was married. Again like Conrad, he was inescapably committed to a writing career by which he now had to support himself and his dependents. Within a year he completed two novels impelled by widely disparate motives. One, he would declare, was "a cheap idea . . . deliberately conceived to make money."[14] The other, he wrote, was "a book by which, at a pinch, I can stand or fall if I never touch ink again."[15] An introduction which he would write for *Sanctuary* was so blunt that a hasty reader might take it as an authorial disclaimer of a sordid and violent commercial story. But that would miss the fact that though the economic motive had been strong, Faulkner's artistic integrity would not allow him to release the book until he had altered it substantially. As Michael Millgate would emphasize, Faulkner said of his revision, "I made a fair job,"[16] not in the sense of a student pulling a D up to a C, but of a craftsman who had labored over an imperfect work until it was reformed.

One character served in *Sanctuary* as a link with the earlier works. Like Julian Lowe, like the Davids in the short stories, like Quentin Compson, Horace Benbow was in *Sanctuary* as he had been in *Sartoris*, an ineffectual failure. Much too close to his sister, much too vulnerable to Belle Mitchell, he was by nature more passive than active, more a thinker than a doer. A professional lawyer and a very good tennis player, he was far happier alone with his glass-blowing set, attempting to create a perfect urnlike shape, than he was among people. He was no grieving faun, but neither was he one of the dangerous heroes. When Ben Wasson was asked if he was the model for Benbow, the onetime lawyer, would smile and say, "I'm afraid so."[17] And I think that we should take this testimony seriously, but I think too that for some of Horace Benbow's central characteristics Faulkner drew once again upon elements within himself. That he made little money when his publisher offered this best seller served him exactly right, he would say, as though in self-reproach for falling below the standard of conduct he had set for himself after the rejection of *Flags in the Dust* when he had taken up his pen with no thought of money and said, "Now I can make myself a vase like that which the old Roman kept at his bedside and wore the rim slowly away with kissing it."[18]

He was now a master of his craft, but with *As I Lay Dying* he learned that in gaining that mastery he had lost something precious: "that anticipation and that joy which alone ever made writing pleasure to me. . . . that emotion definite and physical yet nebulous to describe: that ecstasy, that eager and joyous faith and anticipation of surprise which the yet unmarred sheet beneath my hand held inviolate and unfailing, waiting for release."[19] One of the reasons was that he knew the story too well, but it was also that "now I was deliberately choosing among possibilities and probabilities of behavior and weighing and measuring each choice by the scale of the Jameses and Conrads and Balzacs. I knew that I had read too much, that I had reached that stage which all young writers must pass through, in which he believes that he has learned too much about his trade."[20] At other times he would say of the novel almost off-handedly, "that was tour-de-force."[21] Now thirty-four, he had published six novels. He had passed the midpoint of his life, an artist deeply conscious of his art and at the height of his powers.

Five years later, when he had completed the manuscript of *Absalom, Absalom!*, perhaps when he was contemplating or even drawing his map of Yoknapatawpha County, he would tell one friend that he thought this was "the best novel yet written by an American."[22] It was the kind of self-confidence and assertiveness that would come through rarely but when it did, resoundingly, as when he penned a postscript on a letter to his publisher: "I am the best in America, by God."[23] As he mapped his county, from Sutpen's fishing camp at the northwest to the Old Frenchman Place at the southeast, as he located within his 2,400 square miles the plantation, the sawmill, the monument, the cemetery, and the church (and five homicides), he must have felt an increasing sense of accomplishment. His publisher called this novel his most important and ambitious contribution to American literature. It may have occurred to the author that in following Sherwood Anderson's advice of a decade earlier, he had transcended both the concept and the goal Anderson had in mind. He had exploited what Anderson had called "that little patch up there in Mississippi," and Anderson had certainly been right in saying it was America too.[24] But by now it had become the vehicle by which he had employed the regional as no American had done before him and in the process had reached the universal.

Though he had constructed chronologies and genealogies from time to time, he had done this in no systematic way, so that there would be discrepancies in names and in dates. But he was not interested in this kind of consistency. His characters were horses in his stable, he would say, and he could run them anytime he wanted to. He was not interested in facts, which could not stand up and cast a shadow. He was interested in people, and his imagination still welled up with new people and events in the saga of this county, just as his memory was filled with antecedents that would force their way into new writing as he traced again and again the relationships between then and now; as he would say, "there is no such thing as 'was,' the past is."[25] So now, with *Absalom, Absalom!* completed, with the fortieth year of his life upon him, perhaps he could go on unhindered, a kind of literary Robert Penn or George Calvert, to exploit this proprietorship the way others such as Balzac had done with the worlds of their own creation.

But the publication of *Absalom, Absalom!* left him scarcely better off financially than before. He had first gone to Hollywood in the spring of 1932, when *Sanctuary* had gained him notice. It had been an opportunity to make a good deal of money quickly during hard times. He had not enjoyed the work and he had begrudged the time. Whether he had realized this early how much this work would cost in labor and depletion of the imagination one cannot know. But he took the work, returned home, and then found himself going back again. He refurbished his house and bought land; he paid bills and purchased an airplane. He managed some of the things he might have gained through his writing if his books had sold as well as those of, say, Michael Arlen. But they did not, and so he would reluctantly make the trip back to the coast again. It was good that he could not know when he mapped his county that more rather than less servitude in Hollywood awaited him.

Before the film opportunities, and in preference to them as a way of making money quickly, Faulkner had turned to magazines with stories and would continue to do so. Later he would put them together in book form. Aiming at the *Saturday Evening Post* as he wrote the stories that became part of *The Unvanquished*, he called them potboilers, resenting the time they took from the novels. When he did link them together, he revised not as extensively as he done with the galleys of *Sanctuary* but with something of the same impulse, to reclaim them, to turn them from ephemeral to permanent, to the make the book worthy, in its way, of *The Sound and the Fury* and *As I Lay Dying*, just as he had said he had rewritten *Sanctuary* so that it would not shame those two. Because of financial obligations, because of the vicious cycle in which this pressure forced him to go to Hollywood to relieve it, he was unable for more than ten years to start from scratch on a unitary idea or work of novel length and push it through to completion. But his fertility of invention and the prodigious amount of writing he had already accomplished made it possible for him to keep on creating solid works, some of them brilliant works, during these years. He fashioned *The Hamlet* and *Go Down, Moses* in large part from completed short stories. But he rewrote, supplied connective material, and composed long new segments to turn them into novels.

In the last part of *Go Down, Moses*, he employed a character who had appeared in Yoknapatawpha a good ten years before. In him there was something like a fusion of the two dominant character types. The young wounded hero, such as David, in "The Leg," had been succeeded by an older man such as Mr. Warren, in "Death Drag," an ex-RAF pilot who had trained in Toronto and still limped from an injury sustained overseas. Gavin Stevens was not quite as glamorous, but he had some characteristics in common with Mr. Warren. At the same time, Stevens was a lawyer like Horace Benbow, a man of good family, intelligence, and cultivation. He had more steel in him than Benbow, but he was often garrulous, given too much at times to speculation rather than action. He did function successfully in the world, however, and moreover he knew the county and its people and felt for them as did few others with the exception of V. K. Ratliff and William Faulkner. It would become a critical commonplace that Stevens was based largely on Phil Stone as Benbow had been upon Wasson. And Faulkner had none of the degrees or legal experience that made Stone seem such an apt model. But here again there were other elements—the process of musing on motive or action, on cause and effect, on land and people—elements in Stevens that would grow more pronounced, that owed something to his creator as well as to his creator's friend.

Faulkner had always had a fondness for the persona in fiction as well as in life, and many, such as the Compson brothers and the Bundrens had served him well. Such a figure as Stevens, with a solid background in the county, a major role in its affairs, and the historical perspective to understand what whas happening to it, would be extremely valuable in completing the vision Faulkner had experienced a good fifteen years before when he had conceived the story of the Snopeses, or seen it all, in the lightning flash that had illuminated the landscape for him. The work to follow *The Hamlet* he had been contemplating for a long time, and, increasingly, he felt an obligation to complete it. Earlier in his life he had followed his fancy where it had taken him: to Georgia or New Orleans or Mississippi. Even as he had begun to explore the county he had concentrated on Jefferson or Frenchman's Bend as the creative spirit moved him, but now more and more he was moving towards imposing his will upon his demon, or at least trying to influence him. In the process of getting this very long story told, it would not so much unfold on the page as he watched with joy and something like wonder but would rather be deliberately designed to reveal an overall unifying vision.

But he couldn't start on it then, even with *Go Down, Moses* done. There was the chronic money shortage. He went back to Hollywood, to the worst film contract he had ever signed, to work on gangster films and spy stories and war movies for the better part of three years.

The days when he wrote just for himself were long over. When Malcolm Cowley wrote him in 1944 to propose *The Viking Portable Faulkner*, he welcomed the idea. "I think (at 46) that I have worked too hard at my (elected or doomed, I don't know which) trade, with pride but I believe not vanity, with plenty of ego but with humility too . . . to leave no better mark on this our pointless chronicle than I seem to be about to leave."[26] Now he would provide another view of the county. "Surveyed and mapped for this volume," the legend ran, "by William Faulkner." He had repeated much of what the first map had contained, but now the sense of history was stronger, with dates and with names and places of the Indians who had dwelt on the land before the white man came.

Interviewers had already noted the way Faulkner would sometimes talk about his work dispassionately, as though it were not his. He would in fact say that, after he had finished a book, it belonged not to him but to the world. But this element of appraisal from outside, as from a distance almost, would recur, and in time it would be mixed with something like wonder.

So now he should have been free to get on with the saga of Yoknapatawpha County. In another year he would be fifty and he had much to do, but a long agonizing effort lay ahead before he could turn to that work. In Hollywood he had gone into partnership with two others to write a script and produce a picture that he hoped would make him financially independent. He worked at *A Fable* until, wearied with the labor and the difficulty, he put it aside to write two books that had drawn him back into Yoknapatawpha County. Not only did *Intruder in the Dust* and *Knight's Gambit* refresh his spirit, the first one put him well on the road to the financial security he hoped *A Fable* would provide. Both these books followed a form he had always enjoyed, the detective story. The former had developed from a single idea for a good one, but as he wrote it other elements grew in importance. One was the growing awareness and perception of Chick Mallison as he learned from Lucas Beauchamp, not just about Lucas but about black people. Another element was the relationship of the white and black people of Yoknapatawpha County in terms both of ancient injustices and the oncoming civil rights crisis impinging more and more directly upon the South. Faulkner was criticized by many reviewers for what they took to be Southern propaganda, a plea for gradualism to allow the South to set its house in order at its own pace. What most of these critics had done was to assume that the opinions of Gavin Stevens were also Faulkner's. This Faulkner himself would deny. He said that he would not take the responsibility for what his characters said, that sometimes they agreed with him but they were themselves, autonomous, and not his mouthpiece. Other critics have pointed out that if Faulkner wished to portray himself it was unlikely that he would have done so here when Stevens showed himself too obtuse to learn what his nephew had learned, too unwilling to trust, and suffering to some extent, and despite the story, "Go Down, Moses," from what E. M. Forster had called "the undeveloped heart." But he was still a useful and intriguing character, especially in *Knight's Gambit*, where he was not just an attorney-detective but a man who was revealing more of his life, of his hopes and anguishes, to the reader.

When the *Collected Short Stories* appeared and Faulkner won the Nobel prize, the public phase of his career went into the ascendant. From the time of his moving acceptance of the award made, he said, for "a life's work in the agony and sweat of the human spirit,"[27] he began to speak out increasingly on national and international issues. He was not anxious for the acclaim and he detested the publicity, but during World War II he had felt that it was the responsibility of people like himself who were too old to fight but whose positions gave them a chance, to speak out for efforts to avoid social injustice and further warfare. He did so now in speeches and essays that often reflected some of the sentiments in stories such as "Two Soldiers" and "Shall Not Perish." He did this public speaking more out of obligation than pleasure.

Phil Stone was afraid that Faulkner would feel the completion of the Snopes saga beneath a Nobel Prize winner. Ernest Hemingway had put it more succinctly: "no son of a bitch that ever won the Nobel Prize ever wrote anything worth reading afterwards."[28] Faulkner's problem was that he did not feel that he could return to the Snopes trilogy until he had completed *A Fable*. But the novel continued to resist his efforts and reflexively he turned to Yoknapatawpha County. This time, however, he had exchanged one sort of problem for another. He had conceived the idea for *Requiem for a Nun* years before, but when he began to write it he tried it in the form of a play only to find that straight dialogue was no more his metier here than it had been in Hollywood scripts. His solution, to buttress the acts with the long stage directions setting forth the history of the Courthouse, the Capital, and the Jail, had taken him further into Yoknapatawpha than this sequel to *Sanctuary* would have done if he had framed it as a novel from the outset. In this way, tracing the County from prehistoric times, he was not only moving into it more deeply but seeming also to try to get down a sweeping statement of its history in case he somehow should not be able to complete his Snopes trilogy.

When he finished *A Fable* and returned to the Snopeses, more than a decade and a half after the completion of *The Hamlet*, he did so with trepidation. He wrote his editor, "Have not taken fire in the old way yet," and he complained to a friend, "perhaps I have written myself out and all that remains now is the empty craftsmanship—no fire, force, passion anymore in the words and sentences."[29] But before he finished *The Town* the pace quickened, and by the time it was done he thought he had a story that was not just funny but ultimately heartbreaking too. And he had put more than will and desire into the book. He was in it too. There was more than a little of Don Quixote in Stevens, and this did not surprise Estelle Faulkner, for she saw a good deal of Don Quixote in her husband. Stevens still resembled Stone in his garrulousness, but in appearance he was more like Faulkner, and in the long passage in which Gavin Stevens "already white-headed"[30] stood on Seminary Hill and looked down on Jefferson and Yoknapatawpha County radiating out from it, the County Attorney looking down on his county suggested quite clearly the creator looking down on his creation. It was as though Faulkner were summing up the saga once again.

The reception accorded *The Town* was mixed, and some of it must have confirmed the fears Faulkner had felt when he began it. He conceded that perhaps he had waited too long to put the material down, that it might have been kept in memory too long, that perhaps it lacked freshness. In time his spirits rose again, and as he prepared for the last volume of the trilogy he called Linda Snopes "One of the most interesting people I've written about." He was writing the book because he had always known, he said, "That I would have to keep writing about these people until I got it all told. . . ."[31] This was not the Sorcerer's Apprentice syndrome; it was again another exercise of will, the drive to complete the design or the edifice, not just to write a story that was so passionate and moving that he could not resist it. But there was the personal, as when he described Stevens' unrequited love for Linda Snopes, drawing upon feelings he knew at first hand.

*The Mansion* went more easily. By the time he had brought it to a close, Stevens and Ratliff were old men, like himself and Phil Stone, to whom this volume was dedicated like the previous two. It was more powerful than *The Town*. Like that novel, this one contained episodes retold from *The Hamlet* and now integrated into the conclusion of the Snopes saga. It was the ending of the novel that was the most powerful, in part because Faulkner had returned to the character of Mink Snopes and invested him with a quality of courage and something like dignity he had never possessed before. Describing Mink's approaching death with imagery first used in a review in *The Mississippian* nearly forty years before, Faulkner reached the novel's highest pitch of eloquence. He had completed the last of his planned labors, he said. Now he was free to break the pencil as he had often thought of doing.

During these last years he had moved away from the treatment of large public issues that had gotten into his writing during much of a decade. In *The Mansion* he had alluded to Linda Snopes's involvement in politics and her efforts in behalf of school integration. But this was no major part of the novel. His return to the personal was complete when, apparently unpremeditatedly, he began work on another novel he had thought of years before. He had called it his Huckleberry Finn story but had dropped it apparently without plans to pick it up again. In *The Reivers* he adopted the persona of a grandfather telling the story of his own loss of innocence and initiation into preadulthood to an audience composed of his grandchildren. Almost as if to underline the approach, he had dedicated the novel to his own grandchildren. It seems fair to assume, therefore, that Lucius Priest is to some extent based on William Faulkner just as Uncle Ned McCaslin was based on Ned Barnett and Boon Hogganbeck on Buster Callicoat. However, though William Faulkner traveled to Memphis in an automobile at a relatively early age, there is no evidence that he ever traveled there at that age in one that was appropriated without leave or that it took him to a place like

Miss Reba's house—or that he aided in racing a stolen horse. Once again he had put something of himself into his county, transforming the original with the magical power of imagination in a mellow kind of *ave atque vale*.

How did he feel about the work at the end? He did not know that it was the end though he seems to have intuited it, and had it not been the end he probably would have succumbed to the habit of a lifetime and written again. He may, as a matter of fact, have been meditating a short story as he finished the novel. He had never been quite satisfied with any of his works, he said. If he could do them over they could be better, but each time there was another one, a new one to do. But he had completed what he had planned, and though there may have been misgivings at times in the later years, he had printed only what he thought would not compromise all that he had earlier achieved. He declined to publish early works that did not meet his standards. Refusing one offer, he said he owed more "to the name Faulkner than to the belly Faulkner." And he still had that faculty of standing to one side, or at a distance, and looking at his talent and his work as if it were independent of himself. Seven years earlier, in a moment of depression he had written one friend that he was nearing the bottom of the barrel and constantly had to sift out trash from his current writing. Then he said, "And now I realize for the first time what an amazing gift I had: uneducated in every formal sense, without even very literate, let alone literary, companions, yet to have made the things I made. I don't know where it came from. I don't know why God or gods or whoever it was, elected me to be the vessel. Believe me, this is not humility, false modesty: it is simply amazement. I wonder if you have ever had that thought about the work and the country man whom you know as Bill Faulkner—what little connection there seems to be between them."[32]

By the time he had completed the trilogy and then *The Reivers* he had reached a kind of equilibrium, I think. As more than one reviewer said of the last novel, he seemed like Prospero about to break his staff. As I said earlier, I think that if he had lived, he would have written again, but he knew too that he need not, that the work was intact and that his reputation was secure should he choose to do nothing more for the rest of his life than ride horses, hunt foxes, and read in his favorite books. He had left a world behind him, one he had entered into with an intensity rarely matched in the work of other artists. He had borrowed from his own life for this world and from the lives of others. With an overarching conception of the history of his region he had made it a microcosm. His commitment to it was strong and long-lasting despite distractions of several kinds. It was a source of pride to him and at the same time an obligation to be met as he worked to complete it. He had discovered and explored it with imagination and spontaneity. Later, when his energies flagged he pushed on through sheer will. But he succeeded finally in completing his grand design. He had said his Let there be light, and the place of which he was sole owner and proprietor had come into being. At long last, looking at everything he had made, and beholding that it was good, he could rest.

NOTES

1. Malcolm Cowley, *The Faulkner-Cowley File: Letters and Memories, 1944–1962* (New York, 1966), p. 91.

2. Joseph Blotner, *Faulkner: A Biography* (New York, 1974), p. 462.

3. *William Faulkner: Early Prose and Poetry*, ed. Carvel Collins (Boston, 1962), p. 115.

4. *Mosquitoes* (New York, 1927), p. 228.

5. *Faulkner*, p. 195.

6. *Mosquitoes*, p. 48.

7. James B. Meriwether, "Faulkner, Lost and Found," New York *Times Book Review* (Nov. 5, 1972), p. 7.

8. Robert Coughlan, *The Private World of William Faulkner* (New York, 1954), p. 34.

9. *Mosquitoes*, p. 145.

10. *The Faulkner-Cowley File*, p. 14.

11. *Faulkner*, p. 1153.

12. Ibid., p. 1522.

13. Ibid., p. 612.

14. *Sanctuary* (New York, 1932), p. v.

15. *Faulkner*, p. 634.

16. *Sanctuary*, p. vii.

17. *Faulkner*, p. 546.

18. Ibid., p. 570.

19. Ibid., p. 634.

20. Ibid., p. 703.

21. *Faulkner in the University*, ed. Frederick L. Gwynn and Joseph Blotner (New York, 1965), p. 87.

22. *Faulkner*, p. 927.

23. Ibid., p. 1023.

24. *Essays, Speeches & Public Letters by William Faulkner*, ed. James B. Meriwether (New York, 1965), p. 8.

25. *Faulkner in the University*, p. 84.

26. *The Faulkner-Cowley File*, p. 7.

27. *Essays, Speeches & Public Letters*, p. 119.

28. Carlos Baker, *Ernest Hemingway: A Life Story* (New York, 1969), p. 526.

29. *Faulkner*, p. 1587.

30. *The Town* (New York, 1957), p. 317.

31. *Faulkner*, p. 1672.

32. Ibid., p. 1457.

# *Faulkner:*
# *The European Roots*

I feel like an aging opera singer who has retired a couple of times but can't resist the chance to come back for one more aria. I thought I was through with Faulkner. Not that everything had been said, by any means, but that it was time for a new phase of Faulkner criticism, a more advanced kind of inquiry, based on biographical and bibliographical studies that were neither available nor feasible when I was being educated. I wanted to write some fiction of my own, and I wanted, so far as I remained a scholar at all, to pursue another extremely tough and slippery customer, Wallace Stevens. I find, however, that Faulkner won't let go. The more I think about Stevens and about my own fiction, the more unanswered questions come to my mind about Faulkner's work. I want to raise a few of them here, not to offer definitive answers but to indicate a direction that I hope some of you may want to explore with the help of the biographical and bibliographical information now being published.

The hypothesis I want to recommend is that Faulkner was more interested in European literature and culture, and more formatively influenced by his knowledge and experience of European writing and other arts, than most critics have said or appeared to recognize.

The received opinion, with which I don't intend to quarrel, is that Faulkner found himself as a writer when he took Sherwood Anderson's advice and, as he said in his interview with Jean Stein for the *Paris Review* in 1956, "discovered that my own little postage stamp of native soil was worth writing about . . .

21

and that by sublimating the actual into the apocryphal I would have complete liberty to use whatever talent I might have to its absolute top."[1] Without for a moment minimizing the importance of the "postage stamp," I want to focus more sharply than it has been customary to do on some aspects of "sublimating the actual into the apocryphal," which I don't think Faulkner could have done, or any other American is likely to do, without making cogent use of the European background.

Faulkner's statements on the matter are sometimes more than a little misleading. When one of his questioners in Japan asked him if there was "any special 'inter-play' between you and Poe," he said, "I don't believe so, for this reason—Poe was one of the group of American writers who were primarily European, not American. These others—Anderson and Dreiser—they were American, so the inheritance was more direct than with Poe, because to me, Poe, Hawthorne, Longfellow—they were easterners, they were actually Europeans."[2] That is a logical answer, but, with all due respect to the source, it is a distorted view, and grossly ungrateful at least to Poe and Hawthorne, if not Longfellow.

Faulkner's acknowledgement of Anderson and Dreiser was fair enough, and it often, from 1947 on, included praise of Mark Twain. A statement in the *Paris Review* interview is typical; Faulkner said that Anderson "was the father of my generation of American writers and the tradition of American writing which our successors will carry on. . . . Dreiser is his older brother and Mark Twain the father of them both."[3] On another occasion he suggested that *Huckleberry Finn* was the strongest competitor with *Moby Dick* as "the single greatest book in American literature"; and the only reason he gave for preferring *Moby Dick* was that "*Huckleberry Finn* is a complete controlled effort and *Moby Dick* was still an attempt that didn't quite come off, it was bigger than one human being could do."[4]

It may come as a bit of a surprise, not to say shock, that in 1922, when Faulkner was still in a formative stage of his career, though no longer juvenile, he had a completely different opinion, not only of Mark Twain but of American literature in general. He wrote, in an essay printed in the Ole Miss campus newspaper,

*The Mississippian*, "We have, in America, an inexhaustible fund
of dramatic material. Two sources occur to any one: the old
Mississippi river days, and the romantic growth of railroads. And
yet, when the Mississippi is mentioned, Mark Twain alone comes
to mind: a hack writer who would not have been considered
fourth rate in Europe, who tricked out a few of the old proven
'sure fire' literary skeletons with sufficient local color to intrigue
the superficial and the lazy."[5] He observed in the same essay that
"O'Neill has turned his back on America to write of the sea,
Marsden Hartley explodes vindictive fire crackers in Montmartre,
Alfred Kreymborg has gone to Italy, and Ezra Pound furiously
toys with spurious bronze in London. All have found America
aesthetically impossible; yet, being of America, will some day
return, a few into dyspeptic exile, others to write joyously for
the movies."[6] His sweeping conclusion in an essay published six
weeks earlier was "that America has no drama or literature worth
the name, and hence no tradition."[7]

One might say, of course, that Faulkner was going through a
stage—the sort of stage that Gavin Stevens describes when he says,
recalling his return to Heidelberg after World War One, "I was
a European then. I was in that menopause of every sensitive
American when he believes that what (if any) future Americans'
claim not even to human spirit but to simple civilization has, lies
in Europe."[8] My point is that Faulkner was in that stage during
his most malleable years, before he met Anderson, or publicly
mentioned *Huck Finn* or *Moby Dick*, or invented Yoknapatawpha County. When he did meet Anderson, in 1924 or 1925,
they were both visiting New Orleans, which struck Faulkner as
a pretty exotic place; and he went from there to make his first
visit to Europe itself, where he traveled in Italy, Switzerland,
France, and England, and wrote, among other things, a partial
draft of a novel that he never finished, called *Elmer*, in which he
used European settings and introduced a few British aristocrats
among his characters. The trip and the unsuccessful novel were
outward signs of a deep and abiding inner concern with Europe
and European civilization.

There is other evidence of that concern. I amused myself for several evenings recently by adding up, without the aid of a computer, some rough statistics on the sketchy information we have concerning Faulkner's reading. I looked at three categories of such information: first, the catalogue of Faulkner's library made shortly after his death and the list of Phil Stone's book orders and purchases in the 1920s,[9] second, all the published interviews I could find, and third, all of Faulkner's published works except the short stories and poems printed after 1929. My procedure was ad hoc and in many ways arbitrary. I'm sure I missed a good many references and quotations, especially of European works, although I may have partly compensated by seeing a few that aren't really there. My rule of thumb was very simple. If anything looked like a literary or otherwise artistic reference, I counted it; if not, I didn't—rather like Mark Twain's story of Eve naming the animals because one looked to her like a dodo, and so on. My results, subject to whatever refinements or corrections later scholars may provide, are these: (1) In Faulkner's library and Stone's list, American titles outnumber European by a ratio of somewhat more than five to four. (2) In the interviews, European references predominate, by more than two to one. (3) In the works, the Europeans are ahead by three to one, and a little farther ahead in the early works than in the later ones.

I don't want to leave you with the impression that my survey was casual or careless. I'm willing to predict that more elaborate surveys, based on any reasonable principles, will bear out my general conclusion, which is that, in spite of the fact that he seems to have owned more American than European books, Faulkner alluded much more often to the European ones, especially when his mind was not influenced by questions other people asked him, and most especially during his more formative years.

I looked especially closely at a subcategory of evidence drawn from thirteen interviews, dating from 1931 to 1962, in which Faulkner listed works and authors that were his favorites, or that he most often reread, or that influenced him most, or that presented his favorite characters, or that he recommended to young writers.[10] I doubt that many of you would guess—I wouldn't have, before I made my count—that the author whose name or whose works or characters Faulkner mentioned most often in these lists (eleven times) was Dickens. Conrad, Shakespeare, and Cervantes tie for second place at nine mentions each. Melville and the Old Testament tie for third at seven; however, there is one mention of the Bible as a whole, which I suppose gives the Old Testament the edge. Flaubert and Dostoevski come in fourth, at six mentions. Balzac is fifth with five, and Tolstoi is sixth with four. The rest of the list contains seventeen European items, each with one or two mentions, and only four Americans, with one mention each, and three of those appear in the last interview of Faulkner's that has yet been published. The inescapable conclusion is that the literary masters Faulkner consciously and publicly acknowledged were not just predominantly but overwhelmingly European rather than American.

Again, I suspect ingratitude, especially to T. S. Eliot, whose influence is obvious and pervasive in Faulkner's work but whose name I have never seen there, or in any of the interviews, essays, or letters thus far published. I also sense an important omission in Faulkner's failure to mention, except in one casual reference, Ezra Pound, whose influence was so pervasive that it could hardly be escaped. Eliot and Pound were the most articulate of the American writers in search of European roots in the 1910s and 1920s, but they had many predecessors in that quest, including some that Faulkner may have not considered as such. I think it's fair to say that, if Poe, whose influence Faulkner denied, looked to Europe for his inspiration, Melville, whose influence Faulkner recommended, effectively assimilated more of the European background than Poe did. And Mark Twain, the native author par excellence, probably spent more years in Europe and more ink on descriptions of European scenes than any other major nineteenth-century American writer except James, or possibly Cooper.

Another kind of statement that Faulkner sometimes made will help us, I think, to understand both why and how he made use of European roots. A typical formulation of it is a remark that Malcolm Cowley recorded in 1948, in which Faulkner tried to explain something about his style. " 'My ambition,' he said, 'is to put everything into one sentence—not only the present but the whole past on which it depends and which keeps overtaking the present, second by second.' He went on to explain that in writing his prodigious sentences he is trying to convey a sense of simultaneity, not only giving what happened in the shifting moment but suggesting everything that went before and made the quality of that moment."[11] Which looks to me very like a paraphrase of Eliot's remark in "Tradition and the Individual Talent" that "the historical sense involves a perception, not only of the pastness of the past, but of its presence; the historical sense compels a man to write not merely with his own generation in his bones, but with a feeling that the whole of the literature of Europe from Homer and within it the whole of the literature of his own country has a simultaneous existence and composes a simultaneous order."[12] By that definition and by his own testimony, I would suggest, Faulkner had as strong and deep a historical sense as Hawthorne, or James, or Eliot himself.

Faulkner had made a fuller declaration in a letter to Cowley four years earlier. Cowley had sent him a paragraph from an essay he was publishing in which he speculated on the possibility that *Absalom, Absalom!* might be taken as "a tragic fable of Southern history," or even "a connected and logical allegory. . . ." Faulkner replied that he had seen the essay and that "It was all right"; however, he was moved to offer a more specific and much more complex analysis of his intentions than Cowley's paragraph had contained.

> Vide the paragraph you quoted: As regards any specific book, I'm trying primarily to tell a story, in the most effective way I can think of, the most moving, the most exhaustive. But I think even that is incidental to what I am trying to do, taking my output (the course of it) as a whole. I am telling the same story over and over, which is myself and the world. Tom Wolfe was trying to say everything, the world plus "I" or filtered through "I" or the effort of "I" to embrace the world in which he was born and walked a little while and then lay down again, into one volume. I am trying to go a step further. This I think accounts for what people call the obscurity, the involved formless "style,"

endless sentences. I'm trying to say it all in one sentence, between one Cap and one period. I'm still trying to put it all, if
possible, on one pinhead. I don't know how to do it. All I know
to do is to keep on trying in a new way. I'm inclined to think
that my material, the South, is not very important to me. I just
happen to know it, and dont have time in one life to learn another one and write at the same time. Though the one I know
is probably as good as another, life is a phenomenon but not a
novelty, the same frantic steeplechase toward nothing everywhere and man stinks the same stink no matter where in time.

Your divination (vide paragraph) is correct. I didn't intend
it, but afterward I dimly saw myself what you put into words. I
think though you went a step further than I (unconsciously, I
repeat) intended. I think Quentin, not Faulkner, is the correct
yardstick here. I was writing the story, but he not I was brooding over a situation. I mean, I was creating him as a character,
as well as Sutpen et al. He [Quentin] grieved and regretted the
passing of an order the dispossessor of which he was not tough
enough to withstand. But more he grieved the fact (because he
hated and feared the portentous symptom) that a man like
Sutpen, who to Quentin was trash, originless, could not only
have dreamed so high but have had the force and strength to
have failed so grandly. Quentin probably contemplated Sutpen
as the hypersensitive, already self-crucified cadet of an old long-
time Republican Philistine house contemplated the ruin of Sampson's portico . . . He grieved and was moved by it but he was
still saying "I told you so" even while he hated himself for
saying it.[13]

That statement engages several complex issues about which
Faulkner scholars and critics have not yet arrived at any firm
consensus. Let me see if I can interpret it, without unduly simpli-
fying, in such a way as to shed some light on our path.

The first thing I notice is that Faulkner, in trying to expand
and improve Cowley's "divination" by denying that he as author
was exclusively or even primarily concerned with allegorizing
the history of the South, almost immediately arrives at the positive statement that he is really always writing about all of the
world in all of time and human experience. I think he meant the

same thing in the Nobel Prize acceptance speech, and again when he confided to Jean Stein in 1956, "I like to think of the world I created as being a kind of keystone in the universe; that, small as that keystone is, if it were ever taken away the universe itself would collapse."[14]

The second thing I notice is Faulkner's concession that, from Quentin's point of view, which is the predominant narrative point of view of *Absalom, Absalom!*, the story is about the South. Earlier in the interview with Jean Stein, to the question, "How much of your writing is based on personal experience?" Faulkner replied, "I can't say. I never counted up. Because 'how much' is not important. . . . A writer is trying to create believable people in credible moving situations in the most moving way he can. Obviously he must use as one of his tools the environment which he knows."[15] Faulkner was always writing, if not primarily about the South, nevertheless always and inevitably as a Southerner, and therefore from the point of view of the southern part of the United States, from which he could hardly more easily escape than he could from the universal concerns of the human heart.

The third thing is the analogy by means of which Faulkner joins his world of Yoknapatawpha to the larger world and its longer historical record. The allusion to the Bible story of Sampson, together with the use of the term "Republican," which evokes a Roman context, and the term "cadet," which comes from medieval France, links Quentin's impotent feeling of aristocratic superiority with the whole European experience, from Biblical and classical times on down. This device does more than any other technique that I have discovered in Faulkner's work to make the microcosm of his own personal experience in the American South serve as an artistic epitome or synecdoche to represent the whole of human life in the world. It is his best way of connecting himself to the European roots without which American culture is as isolated, weak, dependent, confused, and inferior as Faulkner evidently felt it to be when he wrote his essays for *The Mississippian* in 1922.

Actually, Faulkner discovered the technique I have just described at the same early period and used it in a prose sketch called "The Hill," which was also published in *The Mississippian* in the spring of 1922. The setting, though not very specifically localized, is apparently Southern—the detail of "the court house columns . . . discolored and stained with casual tobacco" could hardly refer to any other part of the world that I know. The intent of the sketch, as I read and understand it, is to distill into a single timeless moment of contemplation an impression of life that will evoke the whole process of preceding time, and something of the future as well. The focal moment is that of twilight, and the time is further specified as April. The young man who provides the point of view is described as being suspended between today and tomorrow, "terrifically passed . . . and left . . . behind" by "time and life"—not the magazines, but the real things —and isolated from the world of changing reality by the distance from which he looks at his home town in the valley. The quality of the moment eludes his mind, but the anonymous narrator describes his intuitive feeling of it by means of a reference to European antiquity: "Here, in the dusk, nymphs and fauns might riot to a shrilling of thin pipes, to a shivering and hissing of cymbals in a sharp volcanic abasement beneath a tall icy star."[16] This image helps, I believe, to give a kind of symbolic resonance to "The Hill" that is generally lacking in Faulkner's other early work in both prose and verse.

In his first novel, *Soldiers' Pay*, written in 1925, Faulkner uses the character Januarius Jones as a means of juxtaposing references to classical antiquity with the contemporary American, mostly Southern action of the story. Jones's presence, his accreditation as "a fellow of Latin in a small college," and his symbolic equation with a satyr, his "face . . . a round mirror before which fauns and nymphs might have wantoned when the world was young," provide a context in which many of the other characters take on classical identities. The rector, Dr. Mahon, is "a laureled Jove," whose hyacinths are "dreaming of Lesbos"; his son Donald is "a faun"; Donald's fiancée, Cecily Saunders, is a "Hamadryad, a slim jeweled one," with legs "like Atalanta's reft of running"; even the homely Gilligan thinks he should be "a gladiator," and entertains Donald by reading aloud from "Gibbons' 'History of

Rome'" [sic]; the servant, Emmy, hangs up the wash "with formal gestures, like a Greek masque"; and Gilligan characterizes Mrs. Powers, with friendly irony, as "one of them sybils. . . ."[17] The American experience of Europe in the First World War is, of course, continually in the background. The book is more than a little heavy-handed, but it is not exactly a failure; it does embody an authentic feeling of the connectedness between our time and place and the remote classical past of Europe.

In *Flags in the Dust* Faulkner not only created Yoknapatawpha County; he also achieved a considerable expansion of the imagery associating the American South with the Old World, largely by using references to Biblical and medieval themes along with the classical parallels he had already established. This mixture is generally characteristic of the Yoknapatawpha novels and stories that followed. However, rather than trying to take you through a book-by-book survey, which would be a book-length enterprise, I would like to focus on one of Faulkner's most solidly and purely American books, *The Hamlet*, and within that book on the story of Eula and "The Long Summer" of her absence from the County.

The fact that in "The Hill" the protagonist's home town is twice referred to as "the hamlet" may be something more than an accidental coincidence. The hamlet of Frenchman's Bend is presented in completely realistic terms as a contemporary American place, but at the same time it is a place where "nymphs and fauns might riot," and where, in Faulkner's imagery, they wantonly do. It is "a little lost village, nameless, without grace, forsaken, yet which wombed once by chance and accident one blind seed of the spendthrift Olympian ejaculation and did not even know it, without tumescence conceived, and bore—"[18] Eula Varner, of whom the narrator says that, even when she was "not yet thirteen years old . . . her entire appearance suggested some symbology out of the old Dionysic times—honey in sunlight and bursting grapes, the writhen bleeding of the crushed fecundated vine beneath the hard rapacious trampling goat-hoof" (p. 107).

The association reaches cosmic proportions when Eula's brother Jody carries her to school behind him on his horse to protect her from the lust he sees her inspiring in every male human being she goes past. "On the first morning Varner had put the horse into a fast trot, to get it over with quick, but almost at once he began to feel the entire body behind him, which even motionless in a chair seemed to postulate an invincible abhorrence of straight lines, jigging its component boneless curves against his back. He had a vision of himself transporting not only across the village's horizon but across the embracing proscenium of the entire inhabited world like the sun itself, a kaleidoscopic convolution of mammalian ellipses" (p. 113). Unlike many of the parallels in *Soldiers' Pay*, the sun as an image of sexual warmth is as much American as classical, and the classical association is not explicitly stated. However, Faulkner gives us a chance to imagine that, if Apollo had ever carried Venus to school in the chariot of the sun, the sight would have been a good deal like Jody's imagined view of himself and Eula on the horse. If we are also reminded of some of the effects achieved by the early Southwest humorists, such as Davy Crockett's exploit on the morning when "it was so all-screwen-up cold" that the earth froze in its axis, so much the merrier.

One of several excruciatingly sad, pathetic, and funny sequences in *The Hamlet* begins when Ratliff follows a group of Frenchman's Bend citizens around the back fence of Mrs. Littlejohn's lot and ends when Labove's successor as the village schoolteacher, I. O. Snopes, proclaims that "The Snopes name has done held up its head too long in this country to have no such reproaches against it like stock-diddling" and diddles his cousin or nephew Eck into paying most of the cost of the remedy prescribed by Ratliff and the minister, Whitfield, to end Ike Snopes's love affair with the cow (pp. 186-234; the quotation is from p. 230).

Between the accounts of these events is a flashback in which we see the love affair as something very different from "stock-diddling," because we see it from the point of view of the lover himself and from that of the cow's owner, Jack Houston, the widower and still the anguished lover of another former schoolteacher, Lucy Pate. The idiot Ike is a simple, earnest, and, until

Ratliff's intervention, successful suitor. Houston, the outraged legal possessor, is unable to take unequivocal action because he is tormented by guilt on account of his wife's having been killed by a stallion that symbolized his own intransigent masculinity and tormented again by the idiot's helpless infatuation, which is concretely no different from his own bond, or bondage, to his wife. The love, for both Ike and Houston, is real and compelling, although for everyone else, with the partial exception of Ratliff and Mrs. Littlejohn, it is ludicrous or pruriently titillating or horrifying or some mixture of the three.

Faulkner shows it in all these lights, but the stroke of genius that refines it most into the light of that eternity of the human heart which Faulkner always meant to celebrate is his use of classical and medieval imagery describing the cow as the same kind of divine love object for Ike that Eula is for Labove and others. Labove is inexorably forced to return to Frenchman's Bend, even after getting his law degree and being admitted to the bar, "drawn back into the radius and impact of an eleven-year-old girl, who, even while sitting with veiled eyes against the sun like a cat on the schoolhouse steps at recess and eating a cold potato, postulated that ungirdled quality of the very goddesses in his Homer and Thucydides: of being at once corrupt and immaculate, at once virgins and the mothers of warriors and of grown men" (p. 128). In parallel fashion Ike, bringing stolen feed as his morning offering to the cow, finds her standing "as he left her, tethered, chewing. Within the mild enormous moist and pupilless globes he sees himself in twin miniature mirrored by the inscrutable abstraction; one with that which Juno might have looked out with, he watches himself contemplating what those who looked at Juno saw" (p. 208).

Labove's reaction to Eula is that of a medieval Christian ascetic, even though, like Ike, he is also compared to a pagan woodland spirit. Three years after his graduation, we are told, "he was the monk indeed, the bleak schoolhouse, the little barren village, was his mountain, his Gethsemane and, he knew it, his Golgotha too. He was the virile anchorite of old time. The heatless lean-to room was his desert cell, the thin pallet bed on the puncheon floor the couch of stones on which he would lie prone and sweating in the iron winter nights, naked, rigid, his teeth clenched in his scholar's face and his legs haired-over like those of a faun" (p. 134).

Ike's reaction to the cow is equally medieval, but Ike is no anchorite. He is the typical courtly suitor of low degree but selfless heroism who thinks only of serving and protecting his lady, no matter how shrinkingly modest or distantly indifferent she may be, or how much risk he may run of physical pain and danger or of social humiliation by pursuing her.

In the beginning, in the spring of the year and the dawn of the day, Ike leaves Mrs. Littlejohn's house as soon as there is light enough so that he can "see and know himself to be an entity solid and cohered in visibility instead of the uncohered all-sentience of fluid and nerve-springing terror alone and terribly free in the primal sightless inimicality." Beyond "the final hill," by the creekside, "in the drenched myriad waking life of grasses" (p. 188), he hears the cow approaching and smells her in the mist that "shaped them both somewhere in immediate time, already married," defining him in relation to "the flowing immemorial female," the "hymeneal choristers" (p. 189), and, by a bold expansion that keeps expanding, the whole natural world. But he is prevented from approaching close enough to touch her, first by her timidity and then by Houston and Houston's dog, and he languishes throughout the day in "bafflement and incredulous grieving" (p. 192) with his morning vision of her continually in his mind.

I find it an interesting coincidence, and too elaborate to be entirely accidental, that the Provençal trobador poets habitually used imagery of dawn, springtime, and singing birds to introduce their love songs and that one of their favorite themes was *amor de lonh*, or the worship of a distant and not immediately or easily attainable lady. If I read their poems rightly, they too, like Ike, were defining themselves in terms of a love that related them to a single principle of life in both nature, or the world, and the human heart.

The turning point in Ike's affair comes when the cow is

trapped by a fire at the lip of a steep ravine and he runs barefoot through burning grass and weeds to join her. They are toppled by a terrified horse into the ravine, "where he, lying beneath the struggling and bellowing cow, received the violent relaxing of her fear-constricted bowels" (p. 198). She wants "to escape not him alone but the very scene of the outragement of privacy," while he tries "to tell her how this violent violation of her maiden's delicacy is no shame, since such is the very iron imperishable warp of the fabric of love" (pp. 198–99). She allows him to overtake her in the ford of the creek and put his hand "on her flank for a second or two before she lifts her dripping muzzle and looks back at him, once more maiden meditant, shame-free" (p. 200). Shortly thereafter, he takes her out of Houston's shed and elopes with her, like Lancelot with Guinevere or Tristan with Iseult, to a distant part of the woods.

With this success, the universal harmony that Ike has sensed while his love was still only distant worship becomes complete, and the early morning light (light was a favorite image of certain trobadors, as well as of Dante) evokes a relation between him and the world extending underground back through medieval and classical times and forward again to a climactic realization of his own identity in the moment of present sunrise. "Now he watches the recurrence of that which he discovered for the first time three days ago: that dawn, light, is not decanted onto earth from the sky, but instead is from the earth itself suspired." And here comes one of those prodigious sentences in which Faulkner tries—with an astonishing degree of success, I must say—to put all of life and time on one pinhead. "Roofed by the woven canopy of blind annealing grass-roots and the roots of trees, dark in the blind dark of time's silt and rich refuse—the constant and unslumbering anonymous worm-glut and the inextricable known bones—Troy's Helen and the nymphs and the snoring mitred bishops, the saviors and the victims and the kings—it wakes, up-seeping, attritive in uncountable creeping channels: first, root; then frond by frond, from whose escaping tips like gas it rises and disseminates and stains the sleep-fast earth with drowsy insect-murmur; then, still upward-seeking, creeps the knitted bark of trunk and limb where, suddenly louder leaf by leaf and dispersive in diffusive sudden speed, melodious with the winged and jeweled throats, it upward bursts and fills night's globed negation with jonquil thunder" (p. 207). This harmony of universal spatial and temporal relatedness continues through the stages and phases of the day, until the light ebbs downward again. "But she is there, solid amid the abstract earth. He walks lightly upon it, returning, treading lightly that frail inextricable canopy of the subterrene slumber —Helen and the bishops, the kings and the graceless seraphim" (p. 213).[19] Although Ike does not, presumably, articulate his feelings in any such words, the anonymous narrator can render his ecstatic self-awareness only with the help of the European roots without which no American can be fully self-aware.

There is some reason to believe that Faulkner had specific and rather extensive knowledge of the trobadors and their poetry and that he had that body of knowledge specifically in mind when he wrote the story of Ike and the cow. Joseph Blotner has noted that "Swinburne's 'In the Orchard,' subtitled '(Provençal Burden),' may have provided the model for a four-stanza poem Faulkner called 'Aubade,' subtitling it 'Provence, Sixth Century.' "[20] As I have pointed out elsewhere, Faulkner quotes two lines of "In the Orchard" in his early prose sketch "The Priest," and he paraphrases one of them in *Soldiers' Pay*.[21] The subtitle he gave his poem suggests that he may have known the Provençal poem on which "In the Orchard" is based; it is, though Swinburne doesn't mention the fact in his title, subtitle, or text, an *alba*, or *aubade*, or dawn poem by an unknown poet, not of the sixth century but more probably of the eleventh or twelfth. In Swinburne's poem, the female speaker says, offering herself to her lover, "Nay take it then, my flower, my first in June,/My rose, so like a tender mouth it is";[22] Faulkner, after describing the spring at which Ike and the cow drink in the twilight of evening, writes ". . . at last the morning, noon, and afternoon flow back, drain the sky and creep leaf by voiceless leaf and twig and branch and trunk, descending, gathering frond by frond among the grass, still creeping downward in drowsy insect murmurs, until at last the complete all of light gathers about that still and tender mouth in one last expiring inhalation. . . . They lie down together" (p. 213).

Another small indication is that, in one of Faulkner's early prose sketches, entitled "Home," a man named Jean-Baptiste is deterred from committing a crime when another man, sitting on a curb nearby, produces on a musical saw "a lilting provencal air played in a virgin tonal scale, and somehow ambiguously martial,"[23] which brings the would-be criminal back to himself by reminding him of his personal European past.

There were many books about trobadors available when Faulkner was young, of which a typical example is Justin Smith's *The Troubadours at Home: Their Lives and Personalities, Their Songs and Their World, With Illustrations*.[24] It also contains voluminous notes, which sometimes quote passages from the poems in the original language. But I think that Faulkner's most likely source of knowledge would have been the writings of Ezra Pound, who had a great deal to say about trobadors, especially in *The Spirit of Romance*, which he published in 1910,[25] and who paraphrased and translated, not always very accurately, a considerable number of trobador poems, including the anonymous *alba* that was Swinburne's model for "In the Orchard."[26]

One of the more popular trobador stories is parallel in a fashion with what finally happens to Ike and the cow. The cure that is recommended by Whitfield and enforced by Ratliff requires one or more of Ike's close relatives to slaughter the cow, cook part of it, and persuade him to eat it, knowing what it is. The Provençal story is attached, apocryphally, to the traditional biography of Guilhem de Cabestanh, a minor trobador of the late twelfth or early thirteenth century. The short version of the story as the jongleur told it is this: "William of Capestany was a knight of the country of Roussillon. . . . And there was in his country a lady named my lady Saurimonde, wife of Sir Raymond of Castle Roussillon, who was very powerful and high-born, but ill-willed, fierce, cruel, and proud. And William of Capestany was in love with the lady and sang of her and composed his songs about her. And the lady, who was young and noble and beautiful and charming, wished him well more than any king in the world. And this was told to Sir Raymond of Castle Roussillon, and he, being a furious and jealous man, investigated the matter, and found that it was true, and had his wife closely guarded. And one day Raymond of Castle Roussillon found William traveling without many companions and killed him, and tore the heart from his body, and had it carried by a squire to his dwelling, and had it roasted and seasoned with pepper, and had it given to his wife to eat. And when the lady had eaten the heart of Sir William of Capestany, Sir Raymond told her what it was. And she, when she heard that, lost her sight and hearing. And when she recovered, she said, 'My lord, you have given me such good food that I will never eat anything else.' And when he heard what she said, he ran at her with his sword and wanted to give it to her on the head; but she went to the balcony and let herself fall down, and died."[27]

Faulkner could have seen that story in any one or more of several places. Boccaccio used a corrupt version of it in the ninth tale of the fourth day of the *Decameron*. A better version was translated by Stendhal in his *De l'amour*. Pound used it, somewhat cryptically, but with the sentence "It is Cabestan's heart in the dish" to make identification certain, in his fourth Canto. And, in a half-hour search of the Tulane University Library, I turned up seven books about trobadors, including Smith's guide, all written in English in a manner obviously intended to be popular, dated from 1807 to 1912, which contain more or less accurate renderings of the story. Pound's fourth Canto was published in *The Dial* for June 1920, and Phil Stone once told me that *The Dial* was one of the magazines he subscribed to and encouraged Faulkner to read. I concede that Stone was not always a trustworthy witness, but I don't know of any reason to doubt that particular statement. It seems to me more likely than not that Faulkner read the fourth Canto then or later, that he knew the story of Guilhem de Cabestanh from one or more other sources, and that he remembered it, perhaps imperfectly, when he wrote *The Hamlet*.

I would like to conclude by emphasizing the point with which I began, that Faulkner's interest in European culture, art, and literature was not finally a competing alternative to his interest in the South and its people and their history. On the contrary, it was the best resource he had for making the people of the South into realistically believable fictional characters in whom to embody, as he put it once in an effort to define poetry, "some moving, passionate moment of the human condition distilled to its absolute essence."[28] Fiction had a similar purpose. "You write a story," he said, "to tell about people, man in his constant struggle with his own heart, with the hearts of others, or with his environment. It's man in the ageless, eternal struggles which we inherit and we go through as though they'd never happened before, shown for a moment in a dramatic instant of the furious motion of being alive, that's all any story is."[29] That dramatic moment contains the whole experience of the human race, because, as Faulkner said in another effort to justify his use of long sentences, "to me, no man is himself, he is the sum of his past. There is no such thing really as was because the past is. It is a part of every man, every woman, and every moment. All of his and her ancestry, background, is all a part of himself and herself at any moment. And so a man, a character in a story at any moment of action is not just himself as he is then, he is all that made him, and the long sentence is an attempt to get his past and possibly his future into the instant in which he does something. . . ."[30]

That is why even the idiot Ike Snopes, in his moment of ecstatic fulfillment with the cow, feels a relation, which he can't express for himself in words and which therefore the narrator has to express for him by invoking "Helen and the bishops, the kings and the graceless seraphim" (p. 213). So are we all, Faulkner says, defined and related, and so must we all be expressed. He does it well.

NOTES

1. Interview with Jean Stein, *Paris Review*, 3 (Spring 1956), 52, reprinted in *Writers at Work*, ed. Malcolm Cowley (New York: Viking, 1959), p. 141.

2. *Lion in the Garden*, ed. James B. Meriwether and Michael Millgate (New York: Random House, 1968), p. 95. Cf. pp. 137, 168.

3. *Writers at Work*, p. 135. Cf. A. Wigfall Green, "First Lectures at a University," *William Faulkner of Oxford*, ed. James W. Webb

and A. Wigfall Green (Baton Rouge: Louisiana State Univ. Press, 1965), p. 135, reporting a session in 1947; William Faulkner, "A Note on Sherwood Anderson," *Atlantic Monthly*, 191 (June 1953), 28, reprinted in *Essays Speeches & Public Letters by William Faulkner*, ed. James B. Meriwether (New York: Random House, 1965), p. 5; *Faulkner in the University*, ed. Frederick L. Gwynn and Joseph L. Blotner (Charlottesville: Univ. of Virginia Press, 1959), p. 281, where Faulkner, in 1958, mentioned "Hemingway, Erskine Caldwell, Thomas Wolfe," and "Dos Passos" as members of his own generation fathered by Anderson.

4. *Faulkner in the University*, p. 15.

5. "American Drama: Inhibitions," *The Mississippian*, March 17, 1922, reprinted in *William Faulkner: Early Prose and Poetry*, ed. Carvel Collins (Boston: Little, Brown, 1962), p. 94.

6. Ibid., pp. 93–94.

7. "American Drama: Eugene O'Neill," *Mississippian*, Feb. 3, 1922, reprinted ibid., p. 87.

8. William Faulkner, *Knight's Gambit* (New York: Random House, 1949), p. 236.

9. *William Faulkner's Library—A Catalogue*, compiled by Joseph Blotner (Charlottesville: Univ. Press of Virginia), 1964.

10. *Lion in the Garden*, pp. 17, 49, 60, 110–11, 217, 234, 284; *William Faulkner of Oxford*, p. 137; *Faulkner in the University*, pp. 50, 150; *Faulkner at West Point*, ed. Joseph L. Fant, III, and Robert Ashley (New York: Random House, 1964), pp. 54, 66, 114.

11. Malcolm Cowley, *The Faulkner-Cowley File* (New York: Viking, 1966), p. 112.

12. *The Egoist*, 6 (Sept. 1919), 55, reprinted in *The Sacred Wood* (London: Methuen, 1929), p. 49.

13. Cowley, pp. 12–15; ellipsis Faulkner's.

14. *Writers at Work*, p. 141.

15. Ibid., p. 133.

16. *Early Prose and Poetry*, pp. 91, 90, 92; cf. Faulkner's poem "Twilight," *Contempo*, 1 (Feb. 1932), 1, reprinted as poem X in *A Green Bough* (New York: Harrison Smith and Robert Haas, 1933), p. 30.

17. William Faulkner, *Soldiers' Pay* (New York: Liveright, 1926), pp. 56, 58, 60, 61, 69, 77, 78, 151, 169, 250, 304.

18. William Faulkner, *The Hamlet* (New York: Random House, 1940), p. 169; hereafter referred to by parenthetical page numbers in my text.

19. The immediate source of the reference to "Helen and the bishops" is J. M. Synge's *The Playboy of the Western World*, which Faulkner quotes in his essay on Eugene O'Neill (*Early Prose and Poetry*, p. 88), and which he paraphrases in a poem and in his next-to-last novel (*A Green Bough*, p. 16 and *The Mansion* [New York: Random House, 1959], p. 436).

20. Joseph Blotner, *Faulkner: A Biography* (New York: Random House, 1974), p. 185.

21. See my "The Apprenticeship of William Faulkner," *Tulane Studies in English*, 12 (1962), 120; and *Faulkner: Myth and Motion* (Princeton: Princeton Univ. Press, 1968), p. 39.

22. *Poems, The Works of Algernon Charles Swinburne* (Philadelphia: McCay [1910]), I, 48.

23. William Faulkner, *New Orleans Sketches*, ed. Carvel Collins, (New Brunswick, N.J.: Rutgers Univ. Press, 1958), p. 73.

24. New York and London: Putnam, 1899.

25. New York and London: Dutton and Dent.

26. Ezra Pound, "Alba Innominata," *Exultations* (London: Elkin Mathews, 1909), pp. 48–49; "Homage à la Langue d'Or" (*sic*), *Little Review*, 5 (May 1918), 24; "Langue d'Oc," *Poems 1918–21* (New York: Boni and Liveright, 1921), pp. 40–41.

27. J. Boutière and A.-H. Schutz, *Biographies des Troubadours* (Paris: Nizet, 1964), pp. 530–31. My translation. The original reads as follows:

> Guillems de Capestaing si fo uns cavalliers de l'encontrada de Rossillon, que confinava com Cataloingna e com Narbones. Molt fo avinenz e prezatz d'armas e de servir e de cortesia.
>
> Et avia en la soa encontrada una domna que avia nom ma dompna Seremonda, moiller d'En Raimon de Castel Rossillon, qu'era molt rics e gentils e mals e braus e fers et orgoillos. E Guillems de Capestaing si amava la domna per amor e cantava de leis e fazia sas chansos d'ella. E la domna, qu'era joves e gentil e bella e plaissenz, si'l volia be major que a re del mon. E fon dit a Raimon de Castel Rossillon; et el, com hom iratz e gelos, enqueri lo fait, e sa[u]p que vers era, e fez gardar la moiller fort.
>
> E quant venc un dia, Raimon de Castel Rossillon troba passan Guillem senes gran compaingnia et ausis lo; e trais li lo cor del cors; e fez lo portar a un escudier a son alberc; e fez lo raustir e far peurada, e fes lo dar a manjar a la muiller. E quant la domna l'ac manjat lo cor d'En Guillem de Capestaing, En Raimon li dis

*o* que el fo. Et ella, quant o auzi, perdet lo vezer e l'auzir. E quant ela revenc, si dis: "Seingner, ben m'avez dat si bon manjar que ja mais non manjarai d'autre." E quant el auzi so qu'ella dis, el coret a sa espaza e volc li dar sus en la testa; e ella s'en anet al balcon e se laisset cazer jos, e fo morta.

28. *Faulkner in the University*, p. 202.
29. Ibid., p. 239.
30. Ibid., p. 84; ellipsis in the text.

# William Faulkner: The Discovery of a Man's Vocation

In April of 1958, William Faulkner delivered an address to the English Club of the University of Virginia which he entitled "A Word to Young Writers." In the course of his remarks he said that he had not for many years read the work of younger American writers, "perhaps for the same reason which the sprinter or the distance runner has: he does not have time to be interested in who is behind him or even up with him, but only who is in front." Of late he had been working to remedy this lack of acquaintance with contemporary literature, he said, and the book he liked best of those he had read thus far was J. D. Salinger's *The Catcher in the Rye.* His comments are so interesting that despite their length I wish to quote them in full:

> . . . because this one expresses so completely what I had to say: *a youth, father to what will, must someday be a man, more intelligent than some and more sensitive than most,* who (he would not even have called it by instinct because he did not know he possessed it) because God had put it there, loved man and *wished to be a part of mankind,* humanity, who tried to join the human race and failed. To me, his tragedy was not that he was, *as he perhaps thought, not tough enough or brave enough* or deserving enough to be accepted into humanity. His tragedy was that when he attempted to join the human race, there was no human race there. There was nothing for him to do save buzz, frantic and *inviolate, inside the glass wall of his tumbler*

until he either gave up or was *himself by himself,* by his own frantic buzzing, *destroyed.* One thinks of Huck Finn, another *youth already father to what will some day soon now be a man.* But in Huck's case all he had to combat was *his small size,* which time would cure for him; in time he would be *as big as any man he had to cope with;* and even as it was, all the adult world could do to harm him was *skin his nose a little;* humanity, the human race, would and was accepting him already; all he needed to do was *just to grow up in it.*

That is the young writer's dilemma as I see it. Not just his, but all our problems, is to save mankind from being desouled *as the stallion or boar or bull is gelded;* to save the individual from anonymity before it is too late and humanity has vanished from the animal called man. And who better to save man's humanity than the writer, the poet, the artist, since who should fear the loss of it more since the humanity of man is the artist's life blood.[1] (Italics are mine.)

I want to examine the way that William Faulkner saw his vocation of writer, and how, as I see it, he came to look at it as he did. I might have entitled this inquiry "A Portrait of the Artist as a Young Man," except that the title has already been usurped, and also that it implies the existence of a kind of *Künstlerroman,* and Faulkner never wrote one of those. In any event, I should like to ask you to keep in mind those remarks about *The Catcher in the Rye,* for we shall return to them a little later on. For now, I want to consider several of Faulkner's own works.

It is well known that at the beginning of *Absalom, Absalom!* when Miss Rosa Coldfield attempts to justify to Quentin Compson her insistence upon holding him there in her parlor to listen to her story, she suggests that he might want to write about it some day: "So I don't imagine you will ever come back here and settle down as a country lawyer in a little town like Jefferson, since Northern people have already seen to it that there is little left in the South for a young man. So maybe you will enter the literary profession as so many Southern gentlemen and gentlewomen too are doing now and maybe some day you will remember this and write about it."[2] There is no satisfactory explanation for that passage's presence in the novel, at that point in the narrative, if it were not a way of informing us, as it were, that we are presently reading that story. I do not mean by this, of course, that Quentin himself wrote the book in the way that, say, the mature Stephen Dedalus wrote about himself and Bloom in *Ulysses*—to say the least, it would have had to have been posthumously published—but rather that in his role in *Absalom, Absalom!* one of Quentin's functions is to serve as symbol of the twentieth-century writer growing to manhood in the South, as William Faulkner saw that writer—i.e., himself. It is for this reason that Quentin is made to feel the obligation he cites somewhat later on, "*Tell about the South. What's it like there. What do they do there. Why do they live there. Why do they live at all*,"[3] and also why he is made to tell his Canadian friend Shreve that in order to understand the meaning of the South he would have had to have been born in the South.

We do not think of Faulkner as an autobiographical novelist, even though Joseph Blotner's magnificent biography demonstrates how much more direct and detailed was Faulkner's use of his own family and personal experience in his fiction than most of us had hitherto suspected. His friend Robert Farley's remark that "the reason why Bill's characters are so real is because they were real"[4] is doubtless an overstatement by an Oxford friend who recognized distinctive traits of people he knew in Faulkner's fiction and did not perceive the extent to which they were only that: materials used in a larger imaginative creation that was based on the authority not of life but of art. But if there was any doubt whether Faulkner was writing out of his own experience, Blotner's exhaustive portrayal of Faulkner's family background and his first twenty-five years surely dispels it.

William Faulkner, as we know, intended almost from the beginning to be a writer like his great-grandfather, the author of the *White Rose of Memphis*. The extent of his dedication to that kind of career, and his conviction that he would succeed in it, was massive and total. We know that the portrait of Colonel Sartoris in *The Unvanquished* is closely modeled upon that of Colonel William Clark Falkner as Confederate soldier, lawyer, politician, railroad builder, and entrepreneur.

There is, however, one notable difference, which I think, given Faulkner's admiration for his great-grandfather, ought to be remarked. I do not believe that it is ever suggested—and if it is, then certainly not importantly—that the Old Colonel, for all his many accomplishments, was an imaginative writer. He is portrayed as the man of action, of violence, the brave and impulsive soldier and the political and economic tycoon. There is the great moment in "An Odor of Verbena" in which the Old Colonel recognizes what he has come to, as a tragic hero should, and declines to continue the sequence of bloodshed that has become central to his life by killing once again, but that is about as close as Faulkner ever comes to giving him the kind of introspectiveness that one might expect of a literary man. Nothing about his characterization as a Sartoris would indicate the capacity for writing an epic poem, a play, three novels, and a travel book, as Colonel W. C. Falkner himself did.

It is not difficult to explain this omission on literary grounds, of course. The demands of characterization and of the economy of plot were doubtless such that to make the Old Colonel into a literary man would have necessitated a complication all out of proportion to the advantages to be secured. More than that, however, the point about the Colonel and of all the Sartorises, as they figure in the Yoknapatawpha mythos, is that they are the dashing, reckless men of action, the gallant patricians who live perilously and die gloriously. As such they lie at the heart of Faulkner's view of Southern history and his sense of decline and fall; they exemplify the old-time heroic possibility of direct, uncomplicated action that the conditions of modern life no longer provide, and Faulkner's attitude toward them, as we know, is compounded both of admiration and a certain amount of skepticism. Thus the Civil War Bayard Sartoris dies heroically and gallantly in attempted capture of Union Army anchovies.

The fact remains, however, that Faulkner did not, at this point in his literary career, conceive of his old-style aristocratic hero, his man of action, as possessing or desiring to possess the sensibilities of a writer—which is to say, of one addicted to introspection, self-scrutiny, nuances of feeling. And if we think about all of the Yoknapatawpha novels up through *Go Down, Moses*, we will quickly perceive that this generalization holds good throughout. Thomas Sutpen, of course, is the best example: in his characterization there is the explicit premise that he is able to do what he does, build his house and get his dynasty, *because* of his utter lack of introspection or awareness of the humanity of others.

It will be recalled what Quentin's father says about the heroes of an older time:

> people too as we are, and victims too as we are, but victims of a different circumstance, simpler and therefore, integer for integer, larger, more heroic and the figures therefore more heroic too, not dwarfed and involved but distinct, uncomplex who had the gift of loving once or dying once instead of being diffused and scattered creatures drawn blindly limb from limb from a grab bag and assembled, *author* and victim too of a thousand homicides and a thousand copulations and divorcements.[5] (Italics are mine.)

The latter description, it must be admitted, fits Quentin Compson a good deal less appropriately than it does another Faulkner character, Horace Benbow of *Flags in the Dust*. In that novel, to a considerably more obvious extent than the severely cut version published as *Sartoris*, Faulkner makes an explicit comparison between the man of action, represented by Bayard Sartoris, and the man of sensibility, represented by the lawyer and dilettante Horace Benbow. Both return to Jefferson after the First World War, but where Bayard has been a combat aviator who has dueled with Richthofen's Flying Circus in the sky and seen his brother go down to his death, Horace Benbow has been a Y.M.C.A. worker. Arriving home in his khakis—a uniform, yet not that of a real soldier—he is viewed contemptuously by a Marine who "remarked the triangle on Horace's sleeve and made a vulgar sound of derogation through his pursed lips."[6] *

---

* William Faulkner himself returned home in the uniform of a Royal Air Force pilot, though he had been only a cadet and never flown, and limped

Horace Benbow has brought back from France a treasured possession, a glass blower's apparatus, with which he can fashion vases. Here is a description of Horace as blower of glass:

> But Narcissa had finally persuaded him upon the upper floor of the garage and here he had set up his furnace and had had four mishaps and produced one almost perfect vase of clear amber, larger, more richly and chastely serene and which he kept always on his night table and called by his sister's name in the intervals of apostrophising both of them impartially in his moment of rhapsody over the realization of the meaning of peace and the unblemished attainment of it, as Thou still unravished bride of quietude.[8]

The similarity of that description of the vase to the famous urn in "The Bear," in which Faulkner has Carothers McCaslin quote the poet Keats to apostrophize the timelessness of art—"he was talking about Truth"—is I think quite remarkable. The relevance to Quentin Compson's situation vis-à-vis his sister Caddy in *The Sound and the Fury* is also obvious. I shall return to the latter; for now I would point out that in this novel, the first of all the great novels of Yoknapatawpha, Faulkner sets up a contrast, a dichotomy even, between the Sartoris man of action who lives violently in time, and the Benbow man of sensibility who is ineffectual in the everyday world but who dreams of loveliness and creates works of art, "rich and chastely serene," that outlast time, though at the price of forever unconsummated love.[9] The distinction in *Flags in the Dust*, I think, is mostly in favor of the man of action, Bayard Sartoris, but at the same time—and what a crime it was to have removed most of the Horace Benbow material from the manuscript published as *Sartoris*—it was when

from a wound that he never suffered. He wore a Sam Browne belt and wings on his tunic, and an overseas cap, which in his brother John's words "was only issued to our men if they had served overseas." He was thus saluted by American soldiers about town, since "to them it meant he had been overseas and they saluted an overseas man. They turned up their noses at our own officers who had not been over and refused to acknowledge them in any way."[7]

Faulkner could get the kind of sensibility and use of language that in *Flags in the Dust* he ascribes to Horace Benbow fully deployed in his storytelling that he was able to create his major work. In *Absalom, Absalom!* we see a man of action as central figure, but perceived and interpreted through use of the sensibilities of Quentin Compson. A tension is achieved in the interplay of these two kinds of sensibility that is very close to the kind of tension between life and art that Faulkner is getting at with his use of the Grecian urn and Keats's poem.

There is also an interesting conjunction of ideas here. The idea of art and timelessness, on the one hand, is joined to the idea of chastity, of sexual virginity, on the other. The "vase of perfect amber" that Horace creates he calls by his sister's name; each is "Thou still unravished bride of quietude." C. Hugh Holman has pointed out that in *Light in August* the connection is made explicit: when Joe Christmas confronts the fact of Bobbie Allen's menstruation: ". . . he seemed to see a diminishing row of suavely shaped urns in moonlight, blanched. And not one was perfect. Each one was cracked and from each crack there issued something liquid, deathcolored, and foul."[10]

In *Flags in the Dust* what happens to Narcissa is that she marries Bayard Sartoris, but though in so doing her chastity is technically violated for the first time we know also that it is not much more than a technicality, so far as anything more than what in *The Sound and the Fury* is described as being to Caddy Compson a "frail physical stricture which to her was no more than a hangnail would have been"[11] is concerned. For Narcissa has been for some time receiving anonymous letters that are full of foulness. When she tells Miss Jenny Du Pre that the letters make her feel filthy, Miss Jenny retorts, "How can this thing make you feel filthy? Any young woman is liable to get an anonymous letter. And a lot of 'em like it. We all are convinced that men feel that way about us, and we can't help but admire one that's got the courage to tell us about it, no matter who he is." But Narcissa does not destroy the letters; she keeps them. They are stolen from her, and, as Cleanth Brooks points out, in a later short story, "There Was a Queen," Faulkner describes how she gets them back: by sleeping with the government agent who has them.[12]

Horace, of course, cannot sleep with Narcissa, for they are brother and sister, and this is the situation with Quentin and Caddy Compson in *The Sound and the Fury*. But where Quentin, a youth in his teens, is a virgin, Horace, an older man, is not. He has slept around a bit—but not until Narcissa is engaged to Bayard Sartoris does Horace move toward marriage himself. In both novels there is the suggestion of incest, but it has always seemed to me that if so, it is a very special kind of incest, since in both instances what the brother most cherishes in the sister is the technical virginity, the chastity. In Quentin's case the chastity of Caddy serves at least two functions, and I think it is important to recognize both of them.

In one instance, as we know because Faulkner explicitly tells us so, Caddy's maidenhead symbolizes for him "some concept of Compson honor"—her sexual purity means that an unblemished ideal of aristocratic role is still intact. And Faulkner censures Quentin for this; it is ultimately selfish, making a fetish of Caddy's symbolic virginity in order to feed self-love, a concept of family role devoid of real love and understanding for his sister, who has been violated not by a lover named Dalton Ames but by a family incapable of genuine love and trust.

But there is another way of looking at Quentin's view of Caddy's chastity and his grief over its loss, and if we do not see it, too, we will miss much of its significance. Some years ago a very fine student of mine, a woman in her middle years who had raised several sons, wrote a paper on *The Sound and the Fury* in which she showed that while the particular sordid circumstances of the Compson family situation may have driven Quentin to suicide, in many respects the actual problems he confronted were neither unnatural nor necessarily hopeless, but merely those of many a young adolescent. Growing up as Quentin did in a double-standard society, in which the proof of masculinity was strongly equated with sexual prowess, much of Quentin's anguish comes from his emotional immaturity, which has left him still virginal at a time when many of his contemporaries have become sexually active. Under these circumstances his strong feeling for his sister exists in part *because*, overtly at least, no sexual role is either permitted or demanded of him. Caddy is "safe": in his relationship with her he feels no challenge to prove his masculinity. But as Caddy grows into womanhood and becomes sexually active, this line of self-defense is gone, and his own failure to "be a man" is doubly painful.* His memories of his interview with Caddy in this sense are rending:

> poor Quentin
> she leaned back on her arms her hands locked about her knees
> you've never done that have you
> what done what
> that what I have what I did
> yes yes lots of times with lots of girls
> then I was crying her hand touched me again and I was crying
> against her damp blouse then she lying on her back looking past
> my head into the sky I could see a rim of white under her irises
> I opened my knife[14]

What I would stress is that Quentin's relationship with his sister *is* strongly sexual, but entirely latently and implicitly so, and the reason why it exists as it does is that Quentin has been able to engage in it without feeling any social imperative to make it into one that is explicitly sexual. It is when this self-defence is destroyed by Caddy's promiscuity, so that Quentin can no longer

---

* Jackson J. Benson, in an interesting essay entitled "Quentin Compson: Self-Portrait of a Young Artist's Emotions," goes ahead to draw a detailed parallel between Quentin's state of mind and William Faulkner's relationship with his childhood sweetheart Estelle Oldham, and he likens Caddy's marriage to Herbert Head with Estelle's to Cornell Franklin, so far as the emotions felt by Quentin are concerned; Quentin's departure for Harvard is equated with Faulkner's departure to stay with Phil Stone in New Haven at the time when Estelle was to be married.[13] This may well be so; my argument, however, is that, viewed apart from the decline and fall of the Compson family, Quentin's anguish over his sister's sexual activity can be understood as the normal response of a rather sensitive, introverted, sexually immature adolescent to a situation that seems to him to confirm his own fears of being insufficiently masculine.

feel that Caddy is "pure" like himself, that he becomes desperate.

Earlier I quoted at some length from Faulkner's praise of Salinger's *The Catcher in the Rye*. In that novel, when Holden Caulfield learns that his prep school friend Stradlater, who is very much the ladies' man, has spent several hours in a parked car with Jane Gallagher, he goes berserk, leaps upon Stradlater, and begins hitting him, only to be easily overcome by the much stronger Stradlater and get his nose bloodied in the process. Holden himself doesn't know why he attacks Stradlater, but clearly it is because Jane Gallagher had been for him the one girl whom he could love without feeling a role-impelled necessity to attempt overt sexual advances; the knowledge, therefore, that Jane has reached the age at which she must be seen as a legitimate sexual object destroys this refuge for Holden. By "giving her the time" Stradlater has rebuked Holden's imagined failure in masculinity and shown him a world in which relationships with women *must* be sexual. All that seems left to him is his own little sister, a child, and Holden dreams of protecting little children from falling over the cliff into adult sexuality. It is against this knowledge, and in rage against his own imagined sexual cowardice, that Holden strikes out so obsessively when he attacks Stradlater.

The situation is most reminiscent of Quentin Compson's apparently unmotivated attack on Gerald Bland for boasting of sexual conquests; afterwards his friends attempt to understand why Quentin acted as he did. Gerald had been bragging, they remember:

> "You know: like he does, before girls," [Shreve McCannon says,] "so they don't know exactly what he's saying. All his damn innuendo and lying and a lot of stuff that don't make sense even. Telling us about some wench that he made a date with to meet at a dance hall in Atlantic City and stood her up and went to bed and how he lay there being sorry for her waiting on the pier for him, without him there to give her what she wanted. Talking about the body's beauty and the sorry ends thereof and how tough women have it, without anything else they can do except lie on their backs. Leda lurking in the bushes, whimpering and moaning for the swan, see. . . ."[15]

Shreve and Spoade interpret Quentin's attack on Gerald as a defense of female honor; "the champion of dames," Spoade calls Quentin. "Bud, you excite not only admiration, but horror."[16] But what has motivated Quentin's quixotic assault upon the much more powerful Gerald is less that than fear that Gerald's view of the world is right and that sexual promiscuity is inescapable. "Have you ever had a sister?" Quentin asks of Bland just before his assault.

I have sought to show a convergence, in Faulkner's fiction, of the idea of sexual virginity and artistic talent, to suggest that with Quentin Compson in particular, Faulkner created a character who felt keenly what he feared was a lack of masculinity on his part, and to propose a link between this kind of character and what Faulkner felt was the artistic temperament, in contrast to the masculine man of action. With this in mind, let us now turn back to the passage in which Faulkner expressed his admiration for J. D. Salinger's novel.

If we examine the imagery we find that the contemporary artist is likened to Holden Caulfield, "more intelligent than some and more sensitive than most," wishing to be "a part of mankind," but fearing himself insufficiently tough or brave. He is also, I think, just a bit reminiscent of Quentin Compson, "frantic and inviolate," destroyed by himself. There is also the image of "the glass walls of his tumbler"—which suggests not only the "minute fragile membrane" but also that "perfect vase of clear amber, larger, more richly and chastely serene" which Horace Benbow kept by his bed table and called by his sister's name—again the equation of the artist with virginity. We then get Huck Finn, who was handicapped only by his small size; however, Huck would eventually become "as big as any man he had to cope with," and all the adult world could do to him was to "skin his nose a little," for he would grow up in it. There we have the same bloodied nose, and we are reminded that, in Blotner's words, William Faulkner was "five feet five and a half inches tall and he would never be any taller. No smart dress suit or bench-made shoes could conceal the fact that the oldest of the three grown Falkner boys was also the smallest. He was built on the

Old Colonel's lines, but his grandfather, his father, and his younger brother Jack were all six-footers."[17]

Faulkner says that the role of this Holden-Quentin-Huck-like artist is to save mankind from being "desouled as the stallion or boar or bull is gelded"—in other words, it is his artistic sensitivity and spirituality that will prevent the desexing of man, which Faulkner equates with the loss of one's soul. The mature artist, that is, once he grows up to his full size, is as much a man as the Sutpens and the Sartorises, since without him these will become mere animals. The adolescence of the artist, therefore, comes before he is able to assert his masculinity in his own way and before he realizes that his manhood is to be proved in different terms than for others whom he might at the time think are more masculine than he because tougher and physically braver than himself. When he grows to his full maturity as an artist, he will no longer doubt his own masculinity but instead cherish his unique, saving gift.

Faulkner once said an interesting thing about *Absalom, Absalom!* Writing to Malcolm Cowley, he insisted that it was the character Quentin, not the author Faulkner, who was brooding over the situation of Thomas Sutpen. If we think of Quentin as the artist when young, we can see its relevance to the remarks on Salinger. He then went on to declare that "He [Quentin] grieved and regretted the passing of an order the dispossessor of which he was not tough enough to withstand." And he continued, "but more he feared the fact (because he hated and feared the portentous symptom) that a man like Sutpen, who to Quentin was trash, originless, could not only have dreamed so high but have had the force and strength to have failed so grandly."[18] He was telling Cowley several things about Quentin's attitude toward Sutpen. One is that Quentin marvels at Sutpen's sheer strength, as contrasted with his own lack of toughness; the other is that Quentin fears what the example of Sutpen, a commoner, means for the survival of the old Southern aristocracy whose descendant he was. That a nonaristocrat, a man without a family background, could have done and been what Sutpen did and was is appalling, because it is the rise of the nonaristocratic, plain-folk South in

Quentin's time that meant the end of the role of leadership of the older families—the Compsons were being dispossessed by these people, and as a Compson he was not sufficiently tough to resist effectively. Sutpen, in other words, though a nobody, was capable of the dream of dynasty and the strength to achieve it.

What had happened, then, to the old leadership, that it could be dispossessed? Very simply, it had become weak, self-conscious, decadent. It had become Quentin. It was no longer possible to be a Colonel Sartoris, and it was inconceivable that a Colonel William C. Falkner, man both of action and of letters, could be made believable in a novel. Either their latter-day exemplars retain their old recklessness and thoughtlessness—in which case they are like the young Bayard Sartoris of *Flags in the Dust*, born into the wrong time and driven to wild deeds of useless self-destruction—or else they lose all capacity for leadership and action and become author and victim both of petty crimes, sins, failures—i.e., Horace Benbow.

To their place of leadership rise the lower orders, the Thomas Sutpens, the Flem Snopeses, and their kind. Significantly, as Blotner tells us in his biography, Flem Snopes and Thomas Sutpen evolved out of a single character in an early short story.[19] The taking over of Colonel Sartoris's bank by Flem Snopes is the result of this transaction. And we know too, as Blotner tells us, that the real-life Young Colonel, J. W. T. Falkner, had pretty much the same thing happen with him and his bank. And Faulkner needed to look no further than the Young Colonel's one-time law partner, Lee Russell, for a model for some of Flem Snopes's talents at elevating himself, and to compare such contemporary Mississippi political figures as Russell and Theodore (The Man) Bilbo to the likes of his own great-grandfather, William C. Falkner, to conclude that not only was the bottom rail now on top, but the day of honor and patrician dignity in public life had passed away.

But before we write off Faulkner's view of decline and fall as merely another patrician version of the Death of the Gods, an *Education of Henry Adams* for the Deep South such as might have been composed by a Will Percy or a Thomas Nelson Page, we had better think a little more about *Absalom, Absalom!* and about what Faulkner said about it. Specifically, we might keep in mind the distinction Faulkner was insisting on to Malcolm Cowley between himself and Quentin Compson. He agreed that it was the South that was the subject of Quentin's meditations, but "I think though you went a step further than I (unconsciously, I repeat) intended. I think Quentin, not Faulkner, is the correct yardstick here. I was writing this story, but he not I was brooding over a situation." And he went on, after remarking Quentin's grief over realizing that a Sutpen, a common man, could have dreamed so high and been strong enough to fail so grandly, to say that "Quentin probably contemplated Sutpen as the hyper-sensitive, already self-crucified cadet of an old long-time Republican Philistine house contemplated the ruin of Sampson's portico. . . . He grieved and was moved by it but he was still saying 'I told you so' even while he hated himself for saying it."[20]

Faulkner was not, I think, merely making a point about authorial objectivity, though doubtless that was involved. It is true that, if the characterization of Quentin Compson was in part drawn from Faulkner's own youth, one can understand why he might be reluctant to have Cowley or anyone else say that Quentin spoke for Faulkner. Rightly so; for though there was some of the youthful Faulkner in the makeup of Quentin Compson, there was also a great deal about William Faulkner that was not in the characterization. I think of the Faulkner who played football and baseball, took part in dramatics, drew and painted, and by the time he was Quentin's age was already a hard-working young writer. The concerns of this young man, so fully described in Blotner's biography, do not find expression in the characterization of Quentin Compson.

Furthermore, though the Falkners were among the aristocracy, such as it was, of the community and furnished the models for both the Sartorises and the Compsons and though Faulkner himself tended to be something of a snob in his earlier years, it is also true that the advent of the early Falkners and Thompsons into the Mississippi country in the 1820s and 1830s exhibited a good deal of Thomas Sutpen's energy and even his ruthlessness.

It is significant, I think, that nowhere in his Yoknapatawpha fiction did Faulkner attempt to do much with the early Compsons and Sartorises in the Mississippi territory. For the most part they come into the fiction already established on the land, though on occasion there are references made to how they got there. Dramatically it is Sutpen's setting up his house in the wilderness that covers that phase of the Yoknapatawpha saga. It seems to me that something of Thomas Sutpen's strength, ruthlessness, and dream of dynasty can be seen in the life and character of Faulkner's admired great-grandfather Colonel William C. Falkner, too.

The description of Quentin as a "self-crucified cadet of an old long-time Republican Philistine house contemplat[ing] the ruins of Sampson's portico" is also revealing. Whatever might have been his affinity for lost causes, we cannot assume that Faulkner's ultimate loyalties lay with the Biblical Philistines rather than the Israelites. Quentin, Faulkner was saying, was something of a snob, perhaps because Faulkner recognized that he too had been something of a snob. However crude and ruthless and unjust Thomas Sutpen may have seemed to Quentin and to us, he did indeed dream high and work mightily and bravely for his dreams, as Faulkner insists. To assume that Faulkner's sympathies were primarily with Quentin in the matter is a mistake. Sutpen was a tragic hero—not on the Christian but on the classical Greek model—and it is impossible, however much he repels and dismays us, not to feel admiration as well. What I am suggesting, therefore, is that in insisting to Cowley that it was Quentin, and not himself, who was doing the brooding over the Sutpen story, Faulkner was making the point that the patrician disapproval and dismay that came naturally to Quentin Compson was not by any means his own considered attitude toward a man like Sutpen. He may have recognized within himself some of that attitude and put it into the characterization of Quentin, but he was also clearly aware of the limitations of Quentin's attitude, and that too was part of the story he had to tell. In writing about Quentin and his patrician horror over Thomas Sutpen, Faulkner was also sketching the futility of the decline and fall attitude, and he was attributing Quentin's hypersensitivity and overwrought temperament *to* his patrician identity, with the obvious implication that Quentin was the one who exemplified the decline and fall, not Faulkner.

So it will not do to say that William Faulkner saw in the decline and fall of the Compsons and Sartorises the death of all that was best about the South. Instead, he made it very clear in *Absalom, Absalom!* that such qualities as imagination, great ambition, force and strength of character were by no means the property of the well-born alone, and he portrayed Quentin's appalled recognition that a Sutpen, a man of no breeding, could possess such characteristics as a sign of Quentin's incapacity for coping with the modern world.

Yet the depiction of Quentin's character is sympathetic. Faulkner did not undervalue Quentin's sincerity, his high-mindedness, his powers of sympathy and of understanding. Though he portrayed them as going to waste in *The Sound and the Fury* for want of any capacity for adapting them to the world that Quentin was living in, the general portrait of Quentin is compassionate. I have always felt that Quentin's suicide was the crucial event in *The Sound and the Fury*; the family disintegration that follows is the result of that suicide. Had Quentin been able to live and function in the world, then the other sad events—Caddy's separation, Mr. Compson's death from drinking, Benjy's gelding and incarceration in the state asylum, Caddy's daughter's wretched childhood and her flight into nowhere—might not have taken place. Jason's ascendancy is possible only because the one Compson who could have stood up to him was dead. What was wrong with the world was that a Quentin Compson could not survive in the society in which he found himself.

How might have Quentin survived? It is customary to say only by turning into a Snopes—i.e., becoming Jason Compson. But there was another way, which was, by being more than Quentin was, which is to say, by adding to that capacity for sympathy and honor and kindness the kind of toughness and good sense that we see in Faulkner's own character. If we equate Quentin's general background and station with that of the young William Faulkner, then we realize, from reading Blotner's biography and from the evidence of the novels themselves, what the young

William Faulkner had that Quentin Compson lacked—the Sutpen-like dream of greatness, which for him took the form of a sense of vocation, the desire to be an author, and the imagination and self-knowledge that could make that dream a reality. Faulkner conceived of his role (whether consciously articulated or not does not matter) as that of the artist, which is to say, of recreating in language the life, and the meaning of the life, that he saw around him. The great-grandfather he so admired had been writer and man of action; but his literary ambition was not so dominant, and the novels and poems that he wrote had not lasted. His great-grandson saw himself as giving to his writing the importance and energy that William C. Falkner had brought to railroad building, politics, and to his military career. This was his bent, his metier; clearly his talents and his sensibilities were not suited to the pursuit of financial or political or military success. What he could do—he said it again and again, throughout his life—was what a latter-day member of the Falkner family of Mississippi might do in his own time and place: write books that might lift men's hearts.

Floyd Watkins, in an excellent review of Blotner's biography, makes a significant point about Faulkner's early life. Noting the extensively delineated portraiture of the ordinary, nonaristocratic whites that the "semi-aristocrat" Faulkner provides throughout his novels, he declares that "somehow Faulkner got to know these people better than his friends knew them and better than any other major Southern writer ever has, but Blotner develops only brief accounts of how Faulkner played with farm children, saw country people when they came to town, dealt with them on his farm, hunted deer with them."[21] This is quite true, but I believe that part of the answer is that being a member of one of the First Families of Northern Mississippi was a great deal different from having similar credentials as a member of, say the First Families of the Mississippi Delta, perhaps. There was nothing like the same kind of social distancing involved; Faulkner, after all, grew up in a small Southern town, went to its public schools, played football and baseball, engaged in various youthful exploits, and in general cannot be said to have known a boyhood that was im-

portantly different or more socially fastidious than those of most
of his townsfolk. It is true that old Colonel J. W. T. Falkner liked
to make a distinction between political and business relations on
the one hand, and social relations on the other, as Blotner makes
clear, but it is also made clear that his sons and grandsons made no
such rigid distinction. Though the Falkners came out of good and
honored lineage, to judge from Blotner's biography their lives
were not notably different from that of the small town, middle-
class upper South in general, and they knew relatively little of the
kind of social exclusiveness that might have been the case had
they possessed similar social standing in the Tidewater South.
So I am not sure that I agree with Watkins's assertion that how
Faulkner came to know the "plain folk" so well "remains a mystery. . . ."[22] He knew them because he grew up with and among
them and for the most part their experiences were his own as
well.

Quentin Compson is a patrician, no doubt of that. So are the
Sartorises. And I have already suggested that in certain ways the
young Faulkner was something of a snob. But there is really no
contradiction here. Earlier I noted that only part of the life and
personality of the young William Faulkner got into the characterization of Quentin Compson and that the part that did get in
was the sensitive, attenuated, impractical, lonely dreamer, traits
which I have sought to show that Faulkner associated with the
personality of the youthful artist. The early pages of Blotner's
biography contain many references to this young man, small for
his age, wearing shoulder braces, writing poems and stories,
drawing sketches, listening to Estelle Oldham play the piano,
absorbed with Melville's *Moby Dick* and Shakespeare and Bun-
yan, spending much time with his older friend Phil Stone and
reading Swinburne, Keats, Conrad Aiken, and as he grew into his
middle and late teens growing more aloof and distant from his
fellow townsfolk, until he acquired his nickname, "Count No-
Count."

What was it that set the young William Faulkner apart from
his Oxford friends and companions? We may answer that it was
because he was *William Faulkner*, who was destined to be, and

wanted to be, a great writer. One feels sure that the mature William Faulkner who created the characterizations of Quentin Compson, Horace Benbow, Ike McCaslin, and Darl Bundren realized that, too. But whether the young Faulkner was convinced of it is another matter. I have already shown how Faulkner equated the artistic sensibility with weakness, lack of physical courage, and sexual awkwardness and virginity. The rending scene comes to mind in which Quentin confronts his sister's seducer, Dalton Ames, desiring to play the traditional role of brother-protector, only to faint dead away: "I knew that he didn't hit me that he had lied about that for her sake too and that I had just passed out like a girl. . . ."[23] The scene is remembered, agonizingly, by Quentin later. If we compare that remark to what Faulkner much later wrote about Holden Caulfield: "To me, his tragedy was not that he was, as he perhaps thought, not tough enough or brave enough or deserving enough. . .," the connection seems clear. "As he perhaps thought"—i.e., because he did not yet realize that his gift of sensibility and understanding was ultimately no less masculine and respectable than physical size and strength and prowess in the hunt, or in the back seat of a parked car, even.

The probability is that as a young man Faulkner did indeed fear for his courage and masculinity and feel a certain amount of shame over his emotional complexity, and *he equated these with his aristocratic heritage.* They were what had been handed down across four generations from his great-grandfather, and also from his mother. His great-grandfather had been novelist, poet, and playwright, but also man of action, railroad builder, Confederate hero, politician. But over the course of four generations of decline and fall, the latter qualities had been bred out of the blood—so that the oldest son of the current generation of the Falkner family was, like Quentin Compson, something of a "hypersensitive, already self-crucified cadet" who had lost the rough, animal force and aggressiveness that the family had once exemplified and could only look backward and regret "the passing of an order the dispossessor of which he was not tough enough to withstand. . . ." Or so he "perhaps thought" at the time. To be concerned, as he was, with putting words on paper to express a craving for beauty both lost and distant (in properly world-weary fashion, to be sure) was hardly the accepted pursuit of a man among men. By dint of his time and place he, a Falkner of Mississippi, had become a sybarite, a decadent.

Thus the young Faulkner, or an important part of the young Faulkner. The aloofness and "hypersensitivity" were made into a self-protective shield, a mechanism for defense, after the fashion of the young artist anywhere and anytime. The quasi-aristocratic status became a kind of chalice to be borne through a throng of insensitive foes, at once the curse and the glory of his uniqueness.

But not for the mature Faulkner, the artist who wrote the novels about Quentin and Horace Benbow and Thomas Sutpen and the whole universe of great characters who inhabit Yoknapatawpha country. As early as 1920, a year after he returned from the war, we find him reviewing William Alexander Percy's *In April Once* for the University of Mississippi student newspaper and remarking with some sarcasm that "Mr. Percy—like alas! how many of us—suffered the misfortune of having been born out of his time. He should have lived in Victorian England and gone to Italy with Swinburne, for like Swinburne, he is a mixture of passionate adoration of beauty and as passionate a despair and disgust with its manifestation and accessories in the human race."[24] This was very appropriate criticism of Percy, and like so much criticism by young authors it involved the heaping of some scorn upon an aspect of himself that he recognized. Faulkner's own poetry of the period is filled with just such *fin de siècle* sentiments, by Dowson out of *The Rubaiyat*.

The point is, however, that though Faulkner might be playing a role, he had the good sense to recognize that it was a role and felt dissatisfaction with it. A little later he would refer to his early addiction to poetry as part of "a youthful gesture I was then making, of being 'different' in a small town."[25] We find the same censure, much more strongly pronounced this time, in another piece written for the *Mississippian* somewhat more than a year later. This time Faulkner was discussing American drama, and he declared that American playwrights were not making proper use

of the American language. "Our wealth of language and our inar-
ticulateness (inability to derive any benefit from the language) are
due," he said, to our overreliance upon action: "As a nation, we
are a people of action (the astounding growth of the motion
picture industry is a proof); even if our language is action rather
than communication between minds. . . ." This failure to explore
language other than in terms of its immediate utility, he concluded,
"is the Hydra we have raised, and which we become pessimists
or idiots slaying; who have the fundamentals of *the lustiest language of modern times*; a language that seems, to the newly arrived foreigner, a mass of subtleties for the reason that it is employed *only as a means of relief, when physical action is impossible or unpleasant,* by all classes, ranging from the Harvard professor, through the gardeniaed aloof young liberal, to the lowliest
pop vendor at the ball park."[26] (Italics are mine.)

What he was saying here was implicitly what he would tell the
English Club at the University of Virginia almost four decades
later: that the role of the writer was to save men from being desouled by asserting in language the virtues without which men are
only animals. The American writer must use his language to go
beyond the materialistic and the practical world of action into
the human values, what in his Nobel Prize speech he would de-
note as "love and honor and pity and pride and compassion and
sacrifice," without which the writer would be writing not of the
heart but of the glands alone.

Note his imagery. The true use of language is now portrayed
in sexual terms—"the lustiest language of modern times." As
employed merely on utilitarian grounds, however, it is used "only
as a means of relief, when physical action is impossible or unpleasant"—as if it were a kind of masturbatory compensation. He
would seem to be suggesting that he had just about enough of
wan pastorals and lamentations for departed beauty, which he
characterizes as "the manners of various dead-and-gone stylists
—achieving therefrom a vehicle which might serve to advertise
soap and cigarettes. . . ." Nor would he pursue the false heartiness
of "slang and our 'hard' colloquialisms," since that was to ape the

poverty of the inarticulate.[27] (He would soon skillfully employ just such language, however, in *The Sound and the Fury* in order to portray precisely the soullessness he despised: i.e., the Jason section.)

It was at this period in his life, of course, that he had gone down to New Orleans and struck up his acquaintanceship with Sherwood Anderson, and when he was beginning to discover prose for his medium. The friendship with Anderson has been well chronicled, by Faulkner among others, and there is no need to go into it here, except to make this point: that in Anderson Faulkner found a writer he could respect both for his dedication to his art and for the sturdy courage of his commitment. Anderson's background, Faulkner wrote of him much later, "had taught him that the amount of security and material success which he had attained was, must be, the answer and end to life. Yet he gave this up, repudiated and discarded it at a later age, when older in years than most men and women who make that decision, to dedicate himself to art, writing."[28] This was no pale, wan fugitive from the crude actuality of every day life, nor yet another slick commercial manipulator of popular taste; this was the author of *Winesburg, Ohio*, and though Faulkner soon came to sense Anderson's limitations and weary of his unflagging naïveté he had never ceased to admire him, and he closed his tribute to his early benefactor by describing their last meeting. The physical imagery is interesting: "again there was that moment when he appeared taller, bigger than anything he ever wrote. Then I remembered *Winesburg, Ohio* and *The Triumph of the Egg* and some of the pieces in *Horses and Men*, and I knew that I had seen, was looking at, a giant in an earth populated to a great—too great—extent by pigmies, even if he did make but the two or perhaps three gestures commensurate with giant-hood."[29]

Knowing Sherwood Anderson, therefore, confirmed Faulkner's pride in his choice of vocation. But Faulkner was already coming to see that the life of writing that he had elected for himself was not a way of escaping his experience by using pretty words to gild the tawdriness of the everyday world. He was discovering that it was in that everyday life, and in how he felt about it, that the meaning that he had hitherto attempted to abstract into poetry was to be found and that the way to give form to his experience was to immerse himself in what he knew and saw, and to recreate it in language that could define it. To do that would be the most difficult of tasks, and no job for a weakling or a coward. Truly it would require the strength of a giant, but not as such strength was measured in the marketplace or the athletic field or the courthouse square. The strength needed for this task would be found in the courage of man's metaphors and the boldness of his imagination, and the mark of success would not be in winning the girl or building the railroad or even selling copies of books, but telling a story so well and so firmly that nothing important would be left out.

A man's work indeed, as he had seen from the work by other good men he had read. "I read 'Thou still unravished bride of quietness,' " he wrote in 1922, "and found a still water withal strong and potent, quiet with its own strength, and satisfying as bread. That beautiful awareness, so sure of its own power that it is not necessary to create the illusion of force by frenzy and motion. Take the odes to a nightingale, to a Grecian urn, 'Music to hear,' etc.; here is the spiritual beauty which the moderns strive vainly for with trickery, and yet beneath it one knows are entrails: masculinity."[30]

It was no task for a sentimentalist or a dilettante. As he wrote of the Southern writer, ". . . it was himself that the Southerner is writing about, not about his environment; who has, figuratively speaking, taken the artist in him in one hand and his milieu in the other and thrust the one into the other like a clawing and spitting cat into a croker sack. . . . The cold intellect which can write with calm and complete detachment and gusto of its contemporary scene is not among us; I do not believe there lives the Southern writer who can say without lying that writing is any fun to him. Perhaps we do not want it to be." To see himself in the life around him, and the life around him within himself, was not an easy vocation. There was so much temptation, as he noted, to retreat from it through a savage indictment of everything, or else to escape into what he called "a make believe region of swords and magnolias and mockingbirds. . . ."[31] So much of the South's literature had consisted of just such sentimental escape; and such new naturalism as had penetrated the South—T. S. Stribling, perhaps—seemed only another phase of it. Each course was evasive; each was rooted in the desire to perceive less or other than what was there. But if one wanted to tell the truth in language, one would have to face up to it.

This is a vocation worthy of a Falkner of Mississippi. The South was changing. Everywhere around him he saw force and passion, sound and fury. Yet only the externalities were different. How to identify in the shapes and forms now before him the human meanings and values that were visible in the past because of their familiar contours, but which needed to be made recognizable in their new manifestations, if the life of his own day were to be something more than mere action without purpose, motion without direction, passion without fulfillment?

Why, by telling a story, by writing about it. Art, he told the young people of Japan many years later, "is the strongest and most durable force man has invented or discovered with which to record the history of his invincible durability and courage beneath disaster, and to postulate the validity of his hope."[32] Faulkner moved, once he found his medium, from strength to strength, and with the discovery in the late 1920s of his real subject matter, he was launched upon a career that he must have known could be set next to that of the Old Colonel his Great-grandfather's and not suffer in the comparison.

William Clark Falkner had been a man of action who was also, to the extent that he was novelist and poet, a man of sensibility. His grandson, "Count No-Count," would write novels, beginning with *Flags in the Dust*, in which those two modes would be contrasted, compared, and played off against each other in a kind of moral dialectic. His greatest books would each one of them embody something of that tension: he would explore the urge toward definition and the resistance to being defined in all manner of guises, of which Quentin Compson's *I don't hate it! I don't hate it!* is but one. And for as long as this division seemed important to him, his art would flourish. It is only when it ceases to seem a contradiction—when the garrulous, poeticizing Heidelberg-trained attorney who is also the respected county attorney and solver of mysteries moves onto centerstage—that his art falters, and he attempts, just as he said about Sherwood Anderson, to let style alone carry the burden. But by that time he had said most of what he had to say.

NOTES

1. "A Word to Young Writers," in William Faulkner, *Essays, Speeches & Public Letters*, ed. James B. Meriwether (New York: Random House, 1965), pp. 162–65.

2. *Absalom, Absalom!* (New York: Random House, 1936), pp. 9–10.

3. Ibid., p. 174.

4. Joseph Blotner, *Faulkner: A Biography* (New York: Random House, 1974), I, 428.

5. *Absalom, Absalom!*, p. 89.

6. William Faulkner, *Flags in the Dust*, ed. Douglas Day (New York: Random House, 1973), p. 147.

7. John Faulkner, *My Brother Bill: An Affectionate Reminiscence* (New York: Trident Press, 1963), p. 139.

8. *Flags in the Dust*, p. 163.

9. In viewing Faulkner's characters as divided into a pattern of man of action vs. man of sensibility, I am drawing liberally upon the insights of a former student of mine, Daniel V. Gribbin, who in an excellent dissertation, "Men of Thought, Men of Action in Faulkner's Novels" (Ph.D. Dissertation, University of North Carolina at Chapel Hill, 1973), has demonstrated how this approach to characterization is central to most of the fiction of the late 1920s and the 1930s.

10. C. Hugh Holman, "The Unity of *Light in August*," *The Roots of Southern Writing: Essays on the Literature of the American South* (Athens: Univ. of Georgia Press, 1972), p. 155.

11. "Appendix," *The Sound and the Fury & As I Lay Dying* (New York: Modern Library, 1946), p. 10.

12. Cleanth Brooks, *William Faulkner: The Yoknapatawpha Country* (New Haven: Yale Univ. Press, 1966), p. 109.

13. Jackson J. Benson, "Quentin Compson: Self-Portrait of a Young Artist's Emotions," *Twentieth Century Literature*, 17 (July 1971), pp. 143–59.

14. *The Sound and the Fury & As I Lay Dying*, p. 170.

15. *Absalom, Absalom!*, p. 185.

16. Ibid.

17. Blotner, *Faulkner: A Biography*, I, 187.

18. Faulkner to Malcolm Cowley, Nov. 1944, in Cowley, *The Faulkner-Cowley File: Letters and Memories, 1944–1962* (New York: Viking Press, 1966), p. 15.

19. Blotner, *Faulkner: A Biography*, I, 493–94.

20. *Faulkner-Cowley File*, p. 15.

21. Floyd C. Watkins, "Faulkner, Faulkner, Faulkner," *Sewanee Review*, 82, No. 3 (Summer 1974), p. 520.

22. Ibid.

23. *The Sound and the Fury & As I Lay Dying*, p. 181.

24. "Books and Things," in William Faulkner, *Early Prose and Poetry*, ed. Carvel Collins (Boston: Atlantic-Little, Brown, 1962), p. 71.

25. "Verse Old and Nascent: A Pilgrimage," *Early Prose and Poetry*, p. 115.

26. "Books and Things: American Drama: Inhibitions," *Early Prose and Poetry*, pp. 96–97.

27. Ibid., p. 96.

28. "A Note on Sherwood Anderson," *Essays, Speeches and Public Letters*, p. 6.

29. Ibid., p. 10.

30. "Verse Old and Nascent: A Pilgrimage," *Early Prose and Poetry*, p. 117.

31. Quoted in Blotner, *Faulkner: A Biography*, I, 811.

32. "To the Youth of Japan," *Essays, Speeches and Public Letters*, p. 83.

# *Faulkner and the Legend of the Artist*

Who shall unriddle the puzzle of the artist's nature?
—Thomas Mann

My concern is with, as I shall call it, Faulkner's literary novitiate. This is marked by his search into the mystery of the identity of the writer, as comprehended under the signification *artist* or *literary artist*. The quest can be traced in certain figurations of the literary artist in Faulkner's writings from *The Marble Faun* through *The Sound and the Fury*. At first Faulkner sought the identity of the literary artist—to be sure, of himself—as though this inhered in the mythic dimension, the mythic consciousness, of existence. Eventually he discovered the identity of the writer inherent in the modern historical dimension of existence—in the modern self-consciousness of history, or put another way, in the modern history of self-consciousness.

No doubt a systematic, comprehensive treatment of the subject I suggest is much to be desired. I only offer some reflections on it, beginning with some remarks on the evolution of the modern literary priesthood.

## I

In his essay on *Don Quixote*, Thomas Mann draws a contrast between the healthy ego of Cervantes, an artist whose creativity inhered in a feudal dependence, and the melancholy ego of the modern writer, whose creativity flaps wanly about like an ailing eagle in the abstract freedom of the bourgeois culture.[1] But ironically in his admonition to us about the diseased and rootless ego of the modern literary artist, Mann is talking about himself as much as anyone else. Still more ironically, in establishing Cervantes as a model of the artist rooted in a traditionalist Christian society, he is wishfully misinterpreting the actual situation. Cervantes, like Shakespeare, is clearly an anticipation of the artist as "ailing eagle." He creates in Don Quixote, as Shakespeare in Hamlet, a figure of a displaced poet trying to find his way in a time that has become disjointed. He lived in the age when the wholeness of Christendom fell into irremediable disrepair and the modern dispensation of the historicity of culture began: the age when the assimilation of Christianity to a mythic and traditionalist frame of reference became subject to the literalism of the Reformation (and to the even more destructive literalism of the Counter-Reformation); when the powerful tendency of Christianity to become world historical—to assume the secular design of a gnostic millennialistic Puritanism—began to overcome the cosmopolitan Christendom of image, ritual, and hierarchy.

In the ensuing fragmentation of the cosmopolitan traditionalism, which had been rooted in the Christian assimilation of the pagan cultures, the poet—nostalgic for the inherence of art in a unified community—sought to preserve the supranationalism of the old time. In the struggle to do so, the poet (I use the term in the generic sense of the writer: the storyteller, the dramatist, the man of letters) of great talent or genius took on the character, not of a cosmopolitan mind, the image of a polity of the cosmos having yielded to the world of nationalisms, but of a world historical mind. The poet became a creature of history and yet assumed a responsibility for history. It was a lonely state to be in, and one in which he must constantly define and redefine his vocation, or as it came to be ever so curiously put, his function.

In his essay on *Don Quixote*, we see Thomas Mann adding another small bit to the story that he was, either overtly or by implication, engaged in writing—and not less in living—throughout his career: his version of the legend of the modern literary artist. In such an engagement—marked by confusions, contradictions, ambiguities—he was doing nothing singular. He obeyed an imperative of the writer for perhaps the last four hundred years, one greatly intensified in the last two hundred: namely, the writer's personal responsibility for determining the meaning of the literary vocation. Typically a modern literary career begins and ends in a quest for its meaning. It is as if the writer is always trying to give birth to himself. This is the situation foreshadowed in Shakespeare and Cervantes, even in Dante and Petrarch; stated in Donne, Pope, and Johnson; written large in Rousseau, Goethe, Wordsworth, Shelley, Keats, Baudelaire, Flaubert, Emerson, Thoreau, Hawthorne, Melville, Poe, Emily Dickinson, Whitman, Yeats, Lawrence, Eliot, Pound, Proust, Valéry, Frost, Stevens, Hemingway, and Faulkner. If the burden of self-creation falls on the painter and the sculptor, it bears more heavily on the literary artist; for the Western literary artist inescapably feels that he is involved in the essence of the civilization of which he is a part— a civilization founded historically in verbalization: in the spoken and written word; on rhetoric and grammar; on the use of the word and the discipline of the letter. The literary artist is inextricably attached to the expression and meaning of the word in the whole culture, when the wholeness has long been lost and the actual fragmented culture does not know it. If the art of the word fails, the poet fails; if the poet fails, the art of the word fails. In either case, the poet believes that the civilization, or a segment of it, fails. The relation between poetry (in the generic sense) and civilization is indivisible. The writer feels a solemnity in his vocation. That in his quest to fulfill it he yields to neurosis is not surprising.

And yet, for all the solemn singularity he may experience, the writer knows that creativity *only* seems to inhere in the self and that no artist, whatever his innate talent, truly begets himself. In his lonely search for meaning he eventually discovers that strange and paradoxical community of those alienated in the word. Carlyle calls this the modern Church, or the Priesthood of the Writers of Books; Blake, and later Joyce, refer to it as "the priesthood of the eternal imagination." This community embodies in a special culture of alienation what Thomas Mann persisted hopefully in seeing as still embodied in the general cultural situation: the "unalienable cultural Christianity of the Western world." Yet in making such an assertion Mann testifies to the spiritual and intellectual order of the culture of alienation. Essentially it is a secular order, having been in its original formation the arena of letters and learning emancipated from Church and State in the twelfth and thirteenth centuries, and thus an agency of the downfall of the cosmopolitan, traditionalist Christendom of image, ritual, and hierarchy. But the origin of this realm within Christendom dominates the character of its emergence as a Third Realm in the Western arenas of existence. The Third Realm has been governed by the way in which—not as a traditionalist but a world historical order of mind—it has functioned as the center of a Christian and classical (or pagan) dialectic concerning the nature and order of being.

In the eighteenth century the Third Realm (the Republic of Letters, which may be distinguished from the State and from the Republic of Christ) expressed itself, not wholly but cogently, in the establishment of a world historical philosophy of the secular reason and in the inauguration of a world historical science and technology. A universal assimilation of knowledge—this is what the great French *Encyclopedia* represents, the French language having been conceived as replacing a universal Latinity—was the product of a conscious world community of men of letters. They were the advocates of a unified secular dominion of mind, mind comprehending mathematics and poetry, physics and the novel.

But an achievement of unity of mind by the philosophes through an absolutism of rationality reduced the cultural dialectic that had been the mode of the Third Realm. In his brilliant examination of the Enlightenment, Peter Gay finds in the experience of the philosophes "a dialectical struggle for autonomy, an attempt to assimilate the two pasts they had inherited—Christian and pagan." The philosophes thought that in pitting "them against one another," they would "secure their independence." They would attain to "criticism and power." Gay sees "the philosophes' rebellion succeeding in both of its aims: theirs was a paganism directed against their Christian inheritance and dependent upon the paganism of classical antiquity, but it was also a *modern* paganism, emancipated from classical thought as much as from Christian dogma. The ancients taught the philosophes the uses of criticism, but it was modern philosophers who taught them the possibilities of power."[2]

The emancipation of a modern paganism resulted in a world in which all the gods of myth and tradition, classical and Christian, are, as Hume says, silent; and the silence is filled with the voices of Hegel and Marx proclaiming a counterrevelation: man's self-interpreted vision of world history. A condition of mind occurs in which man, employing a never-ceasing critical investigation of his physical and societal environment, postulates himself as the master of existence. But the result of man's control of history—the assumed fruition of the great rationalist assimilation of knowledge—is a specialization of mental function and a mechanization of thought and morals. Both romanticism and symbolism amount to a renewal, or resurgence, of the pagan and Christian dialectic, directed by the inspiriting motive, in an increasingly anomalous struggle for the mystery of being, of discovering a new mode of revelation—at the least of asserting the mystery of consciousness against, as Peter Gay defines it, the modern paganism of rationality.

In its renewal the pagan-Christian dialectic, involving the pre-Enlightenment paganism, the modern paganism, and Christianity, assumed at once a more varied, a more complex, and a more subjective character. Nothing in the manifestation is more apparent or more striking than the fulfillment of a tendency evident as far back as Petrarch: the divinization of secular literature, the conferring on it of the status of the Holy Word. This phenomenon was accompanied by the differentiation of a priesthood of the imagination within the Third Realm, an order centered not only in those writers who were prophets and revealers, like Blake, but in those who were, like the symbolist poets in France, radical experimenters with words and fabricators of a new literary language. Literary seers and craftsmen together made an irregular spiritual government, a polity of the literary mind, dedicated, we may say, to creating out of the diverse contents of the cultural dialectic an irregular myth of creativity, a myth of the artist's self-interpretation and self-fulfillment. This myth has many aspects, but everywhere we turn in modern writings, from Wordworth's "Intimations of Immortality" to Eliot's *The Waste Land*, we find it implied in its multiple complexities. Founded in subjectivity and emotionality, it is perhaps best described in broad terms as an imperative mode of the artist's imagination of self. If the community of literary artists had a supranational character, it was that of a supranational underground of the literary mind which took on the aspect of a precarious order of world historical neurotics. I do not speak disparagingly; the literary priesthood was no place for spiritual sissies.

Admission to this order was not by vote of an academy and assuredly not by acknowledgment of the public, but by self-admission, following a self-imposed novitiate in which the writer strained to satisfy himself as to the authenticity of his calling by a self-interpretation of, as Hemingway would have said, how "good" he is. If the priesthood of the imagination has fallen away with the last of its great exemplars—Mann, Eliot, Joyce, et al.—its primary authority was everywhere still obvious before modernity came to an end with the Second World War.

The modern literary priesthood undoubtedly exercised its power most intimately over aspirants to literary careers when they were tangibly in touch with it, nowhere more so than in Paris. But the power of the Third Realm in the age of printing has been chiefly the omnipresence of the Book and the Periodical. When a young mind of potential literary genius encounters enough books and magazines, he may somehow on his own recognize his true homeland in the Republic of Letters. Young William Faulkner appears quite early to have done so. By the time he returned from Canada following his service in the Royal Air Force at the end of the First World War (when he was twenty years of age), he had, like Hemingway, conferred upon himself the status of a novice in the priesthood of the imagination and had indeed approached the inner circle of the modern literary order. This can be said despite Faulkner's contention in 1925, when he had entered upon the advanced stage of his novitiate, that his first verse was only to aid in "various philanderings" and to make the "youthful gesture . . . of being 'different' in a small town."[3] The difference was real, as he knew.

I say all this advisedly of course. I do not wish to distinguish unduly between the concept of novitiate and apprenticeship. As Richard P. Adams, James B. Meriwether, Joseph Blotner, and others have so well demonstrated, Faulkner served a very deliberate and professional apprenticeship. He deliberately read, learned, and assimilated techniques of poetry and fiction. He deliberately estimated his capacities in the light of his writing experience and regretfully but deliberately abandoned verse for prose fiction. He quite deliberately set out not just to be, but to learn how to be, a storyteller. *But* serving his apprenticeship (self-imposed and yet emulative within the community of craftsmen available to him through reading and, in a limited degree, in person) he served a novitiate in the essentially spiritual order of minds formed in the process of the divinization of secular literature in the nineteenth century.

## II

Faulkner set out on a quest to discover and to articulate the legend of the modern literary artist—to do this in his own way and in his own language through an exploration of the cultural dialectic and thus to make his own version of the myth of self-creativity. He would create himself as a priest of the imagination. If we had an orderly record of his wide-ranging reading, Faulkner's exploration of the dialectic might be traced systematically. The fact is that we hardly need to have the list of books he read. His sense of the cultural dialectic may be deduced with considerable certainty from his writings. It took the form of a decided involvement in one prominent aspect of the myth of creativity. This is the myth of the Great God Pan.

We are very much indebted to Patricia Merivale for her recent meticulous study entitled *Pan: The Goat God*, an illuminating inquiry into the many facets of the myth of Pan in modern times, especially in the English and American literatures of the past two centuries, in which Pan for reasons that are not very clear has been most active.[4] Although Professor Merivale includes no

more than two or three passing references to Faulkner, her eluci-
dation of Pan's appearance in the romantic and Victorian periods
and on into the twentieth century provides us with a sizable
context for the development of Faulkner's imagination.

Of the greatest importance, I would think, is the account of
the emergence out of what I have referred to as the modern
cultural dialectic of a more confined area of this dialectic: a
Pan-Christ dialectic.

The ultimate source of the Pan-Christ dialectic lies, it appears,
in an incident recorded in Plutarch's *Moralia*. During the reign of
Tiberius Caesar it is said that a voice was heard telling a ship's
pilot to announce the death of the Great Pan. He did so, crying
out "Great Pan is dead." This incident became subject to various
interpretations, including one by the fourth-century Christian
scholar Eusebius who linked the announcement of Pan's death
with Christ's purging of demons from human existence. At some
undetermined point this interpretation was dramatically elaborated upon, as is set forth in Paulus Marsus in a fifteenth-century
commentary on Ovid. Marsus is obviously simply repeating a
long-received tradition when he says that the "holiest men
declare" that the voice heard in the time of Tiberius proclaiming
the death of Pan was in the nineteenth year of the sovereign's
reign, or in the same year as the crucifixion of Christ. Thus Pan
was identified with Christ, and the two blended in the concept
of a universal lordship. Of the various versions of the fate of Pan
with the coming of Christ—destroyed, transformed into a demon,
or made a participant in a universal lordship with Christ—nineteenth-century literature stressed the first two, developing chiefly
the theme of the dispossession of Pan by Christ. One of Elizabeth
Barrett Browning's worst but most popular poems, "Pan Is Dead,"
celebrates the victory of Christianity over the pagan gods, Pan
being employed as a summary symbol, and condemns all pagan
myths in the light of Christianity. Despite its popularity Mrs.
Browning's condemnation of pagan mythology, which bears
comparison with the defense of Christian supernaturalism by
Chauteaubriand, represents a minority attitude in her day. The
dominant poetic attitude stressed an equation between Christian-

ity and the repressions of the industrial age. Heine spoke for many nineteenth-century poets when he said "That the gloomy workaday mood of the modern Puritans spreads itself over all Europe like a gray twilight," thereby making a connection between the Reformation culture and the rise of the industrial-technological age. This is the connection implicit in Théophile Gautier's vision in 1852 of the yielding of "Jupiter to the Nazarean":

> A voice says: Pan is dead!—The shadow
> Stretches out.—As if on a black sheet
> Upon immense and gloomy sadness
> The white skeleton becomes visible.

A more complex, and on the whole more important, representation in the nineteenth-century poetic mind of a Pan-Christ dialectic is to be found in Robert Browning's "The Bishop Orders His Tomb at St. Praxed's Church" (1845). The Bishop exclaims:

> Those Pans and Nymphs ye wot of, and perchance
> Some tripod, thyrsus, with a vase or so,
> The Saviour at his sermon on the mount,
> St. Praxed in a glory, and one Pan
> Ready to twitch the Nymph's last garment off,
> And Moses with the tables.

Underlying Browning's ironic assimilation of the sacred and profane in this poem, Patricia Merivale says, is the remarkable feeling of the poet for the psychological equilibrium of Pan as both goat and god.[5] The Bishop's mind as he orders his tomb is poised on this equilibrium. The argument can be extended. Browning's equilibrium, if this is what to call it, is poised on the most significant basic meaning of the Pan-Christ dialectic: the restoration of the sexuality of art. Satyrs, nymphs, and fauns that range through the nineteenth-century imagination—often being affronts to Christian values, as Mrs. Browning saw—belong to the impulse to rediscover through artistic vision the mythical basis of culture in the biology of male and female, and the variations thereof. The same crisis of meaning in the Christian conception of history that called for the elevation of Christ over Pan in the Pan-Christ dialectic, we are led to reflect, provoked the appearance of world historical minds like Friedrich Nietzsche and Sigmund Freud.

Once the sexuality of art began to be comprehended in a much broader perspective of a sexuality of history, the Pan-Christ dialectic receded in poetry. It did, however, find continuing expression in prose fiction, its most vivid expositor being D. H. Lawrence. Lawrence, notably in his later career, made a rather literal identification between the Pan-Christ dialectic and the nature of the artist. This can be illustrated merely by looking at a painting by Dorothy Brett, in which Lawrence is portrayed as both Christ on the Cross and Pan. Seated on a rock, his usual resting place, Pan is looking at Christ, his hoofed hands upraised. What is even more intriguing is that Lawrence himself painted a similar picture.[6] In this stage the Pan-Christ dialectic reaches an absurd yet profound impasse. The pagan goat god and the crucified virgin God are viewed as an ultimate duality—which is the ultimate mystery—of the literary artist. The view represents an apotheosis of the ego of the individual artist, but the summation exists in an unresolved and, it would seem, unresolvable tension in the myth of creativity. The rebellion in art against the rationalistic modernity cannot reconcile its sources in a vision of man's destiny grounded in historical revelation and an earlier vision rooted in a cosmological mythology.

These visions form an apposition in the early stage of Faulkner's literary novitiate as this is represented by *The Marble Faun*, a college play, and various sketches and short stories.

A pastoral poem in structure, *The Marble Faun* is more ambitious than has ordinarily been recognized. A parallel to, possibly an anticipation of Eliot's *The Waste Land* (some of the individual poems in Faulkner's first book were written before 1920, although the book was not published until 1924), *The Marble Faun* is based on nothing less than an intention to express the modern cultural dialectic, and it attains a considerable complexity of meaning. The faun, a creature of Pan and a figure of the modern poet, speaks out of his imprisonment in a work of art, a statue of a faun set in a formal garden. Of indeterminate location, the garden represents the lapsarian garden of modernity, in which significantly "that quick keen snake/Is free to come and go" but the faun is forever "marble-bound." His bondage is subtly related to the freedom of the snake, inasmuch as the faun in order to imagine a furtive glimpse of Pan must "glide . . . like a snake" to peer into a glade where Pan sits on a rock brooding beside a hushed pool. The faun's consciousness of the snake—the biblical snake who destroyed the cosmological innocence of the first garden—is allied to his awareness of his desire "For things I know, yet cannot know." These would include the whole cyclical sequence of the seasons, the joys and the sadnesses of the natural progression from birth to death—spring, summer, autumn, winter. The introverted longing for the world that responded to the piping of Pan is associated not only with the frustration symbolized by the snake in the garden but by the intrusion into the garden of the arty people who pause to admire the statue of the faun and by the dancers who at night beneath paper lanterns move ungracefully "To brass horns horrible and loud."[7] These intruders, we might say, are "modern pagans." Eliot would call them the "hollow men." The corruption of the natural world by a Christianity that is in alliance with the modern philosophy of the machine society—to a quite discernible extent Faulkner succeeds in embodying something like this vision in his first work. More significantly, he does so through a complex perspective: the faun's tormented consciousness of being conscious. Thus he creates in the faun's sense of the dispossession of Pan an emblem of the suffering induced by the solipsistic state.

Despite his complexity of point of view in *The Marble Faun*, Faulkner opposes the classical myth to Christianity and to modernity with almost no emphasis on the motive that is fundamental in the literary critique of modernity, the depletion of the sexual basis of culture. But in his next work, an unpublished one-act play entitled *The Marionettes*, Faulkner boldly engages the sexual theme. (Actually, according to Noel Polk in his careful study of the manuscript of the play, this engagement is forecast in a contemplated but discarded version of *The Marble Faun*. In *The Marionettes*, Faulkner again presents the displacement of the pagan garden of fecundity and the imprisonment of the natural or instinctual in a formal garden. The image of Pan appears in a statue of a faun, like the one in *The Marble Faun*. But what occurs in the garden—the frustration of the truth of art and the integrity of the artist—is symbolized in the impotent lust of Pierrot and the delight in meretricious adornment on the part of Marietta. The rape of Marietta—Pierrot's dream of raping her—is a depreciation of the sexuality of the human spirit as this is represented in the legend of Pan the ravisher of nymphs. In *The Marionettes* the contrast between the mythic world of the goat god and the sterile world of modernity is drawn far more graphically than the contrast between Arcadia and modernity in *The Marble Faun*, and in Pierrot as a figure of the poet we get something approaching the terror and violence inherent in psychic repression. This is enhanced by the suggestion that the psychic aggression of Pierrot against Marietta is against himself, that, as a matter of fact, the two are aspects of the same condition of spirit.[8] The Pierrot-Marietta relationship foreshadows the obsessive concern Faulkner was to develop with the ambiguities of the masculine and feminine duality in life and in art.

How thoroughly the young Faulkner's imagination of the poet was being caught up in the question of the sexuality of art becomes clear in "Nympholepsy." Unpublished until recently (when Mr. Meriwether brought it into print), this sketch is an expansion, done in early 1925, of a sketch entitled "The Hill" published in 1922 in *The Mississippian*. In both the first and second versions of this strange little piece, Faulkner finds his protagonist in a youthful wanderer and dreamer. He resembles Faulkner himself in disposition, although the indication is that he is likely a Midwestern youth, an itinerant farm laborer who is following thresher crews northward with the wheat harvest. After a day's harvesting, which offers the usual prospect of "cloddish eating, and dull sleep in a casual rooming house," the youth is hoping that "a girl like defunctive music, moist with heat, in blue gingham, would cross his path." But when he dimly glimpses a feminine figure and begins to pursue her, she turns out to be no blue-gingham country girl. In an increasingly furious chase after this elusive creature, he slips into a dark stream and, nearly drowning, feels the touch of a "swift leg" and the "point of a breast." Then he sees "her swing herself, dripping, upon the bank." But his further pursuit of the creature—"her body, ghostly in the moonless dusk, mounting the hill"—is futile. He is left to wonder in despair: "But I touched her." And to return to labor another day surrounded by "all the old despairs of time and breath." In depicting the experience of demoniac possession by a nymph (common enough in ancient times), Faulkner explicitly identifies the theme of the psychic repression of the poet, or artist, with the Calvinistic work-ethic society. This is made more explicit by certain symbols employed in the sketch, especially the church spire and the courthouse. Both in the protagonist and in the setting of "Nympholepsy" Faulkner for the first time locates the pagan-Christian dialect on the American scene and more or less definitely associates it with his own quest for vocation.[9]

Presumably at about the same time he revised "The Hill" as "Nympholepsy," Faulkner wrote a sketch of greater import in his literary novitiate than anything he had set down before. Entitled "Out of Nazareth," this was published in the New Orleans *Picayune* on Easter Sunday, 1925. One of several sketches he contributed to the *Picayune* during the period he lived in the New Orleans French Quarter (the first six months of 1925), "Out of Nazareth" is clearly intended, as Carvel Collins has said, to infer a parallel between its protagonist, another wandering youth, and the figure of the young Christ. Seventeen years old he has left his home town in the Midwest; with no destination in mind he lives indifferently by himself or among other wanderers, enjoying a sense of peace and at oneness with nature and man. Eventually he comes to New Orleans, where one morning in Jackson Square he is seen by Faulkner and his friend William Spratling, the painter, standing "beneath sparrows delirious in a mimosa," against the background of "a vague Diana in torturous escape from marble draperies." The youth's face is brooding upon the spire of St. Louis Cathedral, or perhaps "something in the sky." Spratling exclaims, "My God, look at that face."

And one could imagine young David looking like that. One could imagine Jonathan getting that look from David, and, serving that highest function of which sorry man is capable, being the two of them beautiful in similar peace and simplicity —beautiful as gods, as no woman can ever be. And to think of speaking to him, of entering that dream, was like a desecration.

But when the marvelous youth—Faulkner calls him David, but the youth never gives his name himself—responds to their attention with a hello, they take him to lunch, finding out among other things that he has a "battered 'Shropshire Lad' " (acquired by chance) and that he has written a story about his journeying. In the sketch Faulkner presents David's account without alteration. It is a very simple report of the youth's experiences on the road, save for a touch here and there of attempts at literary style. "Some of the words mean nothing, as far as I know," Faulkner comments. Then he adds parenthetically "and words are my meat and bread and drink." But to change David's words "would be to destroy David himself."

As Carvel Collins points out, David suggests a representation of the young Jesus. The title of the sketch, its publication on Easter Sunday, the name David given the youth by Faulkner ("I am the root and offspring of David, and the bright and morning star." Rev. 22.16.), such details as the youth's fondness for sleeping in hay with cattle, together with the emphasis that in a virginal purity and innocence he is "serving his appointed ends" confirm the relation of the youth to Jesus. A more profound motive in the sketch although hardly less obvious, I think, is Faulkner's association of the young Jesus with his own search for the meaning of the vocation to which by this time he had come to feel a complete commitment.

In "Out of Nazareth" the pagan element in the cultural dialectic is subordinated. David appears against the background of Diana, the goddess of chastity. His eyes look heavenward; he leaves a message of hope about the ordinary people he has met in his wandering. The message may have literary flaws and unknown words in it, but it is sacramental. It is the authentic expression of

David. Faulkner distinctly symbolizes the implication of Christ in the mystery of the writer's vocation and, to be sure, relates the implication to the identity of a writer who had come out of Oxford, Mississippi, and who, as David says about himself in the story, might someday return to his home town, the place of his nativity.[10]

So far as I am aware no writer, and certainly not Faulkner, became so literally involved in an image of the writer drawn from the Pan-Christ dialectic as did Lawrence. But the Lawrentian extreme points up the importance of the visionary source of the modern literary vocation in a pagan-Christian opposition and reconciliation. And there are, interestingly enough, two related short stories by Faulkner, written probably in the mid-1920s, that suggest Lawrence. Both are about the same character, Wilfred Midgleston, a former draughtsman for a New York architectural firm. In "Black Music" the narrator encounters Midgleston in a Caribbean port named Rincon, where as an old man he lives a barfly existence, sleeping in an attic in a roll of tarred roofing paper. In the story he recounts to the narrator, he tells how he was transformed by the god Pan into a faun. He existed in this transformed state for one day, when he is used by Pan to frighten Mrs. Van Dyming, wealthy patroness of the arts, from her Virginia estate. The arty matron has planned to build a replica of a Roman theatre on the site of a stand of native grape vines. Midgleston, whose purpose in going to Virginia had been to consult with Mrs. Van Dyming about plans for the theatre, flees to the Caribbean island and remains there, a true believer in Pan. If "the Bible says them little men were myths," Midgleston knows differently.[11] The comic mode of "Black Music" is countered by the surrealistic poetry of "Carcassonne," the second story about Midgleston. Rolled up in his tar paper bed, the old man becomes pure poetic consciousness. He is "on a buckskin pony with eyes like blue electricity and a mane like tangled fire, galloping up the hill right off into the high heaven of the world." The ecstatic flight is mingled with images of the medieval crusades (knights "riding against the assembled foes of our meek Lord"); of the Crucifixion ("But somebody always killed the first rate riders");

of the Resurrection; and of the "dark and tragic figure of the Earth, his mother." The theme of Faulkner's surrealistic elaboration of an analogy between poetry and Christianity seems to be stated in the declaration, "*I want to perform something bold and tragical and austere.*"[12] To be a first rate rider is to be crucified for it. Faulkner apparently seeks to depict in Midgleston both the pathos of a defeated poet and the ironic victory of his imagination.

### III

The decisive stage of Faulkner's literary novitiate may be traced in the unfoldment of the legend of the artist in the increasingly complex and subtle interplay of classical paganism, modern paganism, and Christianity in *Soldiers' Pay, Mosquitoes, Flags in the Dust,* and *The Sound and the Fury.* This evolution, I realize, cannot here be set forth in the detail required for satisfactory analysis. I shall attempt a partial outline.

In *Soldiers' Pay,* Faulkner creates the dialectical interplay chiefly through the relationships among three characters: Donald Mahon, the First World War pilot who has been shot down over Flanders, and horribly scarred and in a comatose state, is returned to his small-town home in Georgia to die; Donald's father, the Reverend Mr. Mahon, rector of the Episcopal Church in the community, an outwardly professing Christian, who is no longer, if he ever was, an inwardly believing one; and Januarius Jones, described as "a late fellow of Latin in a small college," a brash, enigmatic person who just shows up one April day at the rector's garden gate. All three of these characters bear the mark of Pan. Before the war Donald has run naked in the moonlight and made love to Emmy, the servant girl, whom he transformed, so to speak, into a nymph. Donald, a devotee of "A Shropshire Lad," is a figure of the poet as faun, and bearing his battle scar he is a sacrificial victim, a type of the wounded and dying god. The rector has one great passion, a beautiful rose bush in his garden. He awaits its first bloom with the impatience of a young man expecting his mistress, and the blooming rose brings him an ecstasy like that known to "the old pagan who kept his Byzantine goblet at his bedside and slowly wore away the rim kissing it." Jones is a satyr. Grossly sensual, forever in a state of "nympholepsy," and would-be seducer both of Emmy and Cecily, Donald's intended, he is suggestive of the Pan who became satanic at the time of Christ's crucifixion and may be taken as the demonic inverse of Donald Mahon. Jones finally accomplishes his seduction of Emmy while the service for the burial of the dead being said over Donald echoes in her mind ("I am the Resurrection and the Life, saith the Lord. . . .") and taps sound distantly from a local Boy Scout's bugle. *Soldiers' Pay* ends with rector standing outside a shabby Negro church, which has a "canting travesty of a spire," listening to "the crooning submerged passion of the dark race," who have made a "personal Father" out of the white man's "remote God." Then he takes his way back "along the mooned land inevitable with to-morrow and sweat, with sex and death and damnation." In *Soldiers' Pay* there is creative passion left neither in classical paganism nor in Christianity. Only the alien dark race has any harmony with existence. To a certain extent Faulkner succeeds in dramatizing in terms of the life in a little Georgia town a post-pagan, and post-Christian, wasteland. The central figure in this world is the Reverend Mr. Mahon. A lapsed Christian and frustrated pagan strolling his formal garden, in love with a perfected symbol of love, his beautiful rose, the rector, a literary person if not a writer, is a figure in the priesthood of art. A humanitarian deist, or, it could be, a total skeptic, though he would never say so, he evokes a type of the modern literary sensibility. A type of modern pagan, representing the defeat of the poetic imagination in modernity, he is imprisoned in his garden like the marbleized faun; or, to use his image of the ecstasy of art, he is sealed in a Byzantine vase of surpassing beauty. Save for certain intimations of their viability in Donald, both Pan and Christ are dead in the world of *Soldiers' Pay*.[13]

But Faulkner's imagination of the condition of the artist's imagination in modernity did not reach an impasse in *Soldiers' Pay*. On the contrary, his first novel marks its considerable expansion and complication, in nothing more so than in the way in which the dialectical interplay in the story establishes the action and the symbols of a relationship between the sexuality of art and the sexuality of the human community as represented in time and place by Charlestown, Georgia.

In *Mosquitoes*, Faulkner might well seem to have contemplated something like a full-scale approach through classical myth to the meaning of the artist's nature in the modern age. The outstanding theme of the novel announces itself clearly in the beginning as the sexuality of art and the artist. It is never certain whether Gordon, the French Quarter sculptor, who worships his own abstract statue of a virgin, or Mrs. Maurier, the wealthy patroness of art, whose yacht, the *Nausikka* is named for the virgin Nausicca in the *Odyssey* and whose own condition, as it turns out, is that of a psychic, if not technical, virginity, is the chief character in the novel. The exploration of the sexual motivation of creativity, or the lack of it, is ruthlessly pursued by Faulkner in a talky comedy about a mixed bag of New Orleans artists and wealthy and petty bourgeoisie who embark on the *Nausikka* for a trivial and aborted little cosmological odyssey around Lake Pontchartrain. Faulkner weaves into his drama a whole complex of references and allusions to the classical myths dealing with the sexual nature of man. He even brings himself in briefly as a dark faunal little man who is a "liar by profession" and, it is implied, a bit of a goat. But the central insistence in *Mosquitoes* is Christian. Gordon, who is described as having a "faunlike face" and in various ways is associated with "pipes" and "centaurs' hooves," finds his basic meaning in his having suffered the somewhat obscure but poignant "autogethsemane" that his abstraction of the virginal girl—a torso only, headless, armless, legless—represents. Mrs. Maurier in part resembles the Nausicca of Joyce's *Ulysses* (Gertie McDowell, the devotee of pseudo-art), in part the innocent Nausicca of the *Odyssey*, who has her first, and possibly only, awakening to love in her impossible longing for Ulysses. Gordon intuits the suffering behind the masked face of Mrs. Maurier and makes a clay molding of her face "that exposed her face for the mask it was, and still more, a mask unaware." Julius Kauffman, called "the Semitic man'" throughout the novel,

explains the history of Mrs. Maurier to the provincial Dawson
Fairchild, a novelist who resembles Sherwood Anderson. In effect
in giving a very specific account of Mrs. Maurier's marriage of
convenience to a man twice her age—a former plantation overseer and a rank and crafty opportunist—the Semitic man establishes her character in specific historical and social circumstances.
The story Kauffman tells is in fact, Blotner shows, based on one
told about a young lady in Oxford, Mississippi. Although the
introduction of this kind of historical specification into *Mosquitoes* may be reckoned to be awkward and to further increase its
disparate quality, it points to the major direction Faulkner's dialectical apprehension of the ground of art and the character of
the artist was beginning to take. This is to say, toward the historicity of art. Further evidence of this is provided in the best known
scene in *Mosquitoes*; usually compared to the Circe episode in
*Ulysses*, this is the episode following the scene in Gordon's studio
where Kauffman relates the story about Mrs. Maurier—a surrealistic scene in which the Semitic man delivers a description
of genius as "that Passion Week of the heart." He refers to Dante,
who "invented Beatrice, creating himself a maid that life had not
had time to create, and laid upon her frail and unbowed shoulders
the whole burden of man's history of his impossible heart's
desire." The poet's creation of a figure to bear the weight of the
burdened history of impossible desires of the human heart: Beatrice suggests the Christian sense of the primacy of history—the
unredeemed history of the human heart in conflict with itself,
the source Faulkner would say twenty-five years later of all
storytelling.[14] In Kauffman, Faulkner came into the understanding
that art is a part of history—the understanding that is implied
in Gordon's intuition of the meaning of Mrs. Maurier's face and
that Kauffman explicates. It is to be noted that both Kauffman,
the Semitic man, and his sister Eva are significant figurations of
the poet in *Mosquitoes*. Faulkner ascribes some of his own poems
to the latter, including an important one called "Hermaphroditis." This poem is a comment on the legend of Hermaphroditis
and Salmacis, the nymph, who after Hermaphroditis bathes in her
pool, desires him, is rebuffed, and following the nymph's appeal

to the gods is forever joined to her. Eva is either an active or latent lesbian; it is not clear which. But either way she descends from Sappho of Lesbos and is in her modern guise a world historical poetess. Her brother is a younger version of the "Wealthy Jew" in the *New Orleans Sketches*, a poetic apostrophe to the type of the world historical Jew, who says to the gentiles, "No soil is foreign to my people, for have we not conquered all lands with the story of your Nativity?"[15]

In his attempt to explore the sexuality of art in *Mosquitoes*, Faulkner sighted a momentous subject. This is the modern concept of the historical nature of sexuality. Under this concept the sexuality of individuals and families is viewed as inherent in the process of history. Under the dominion of history all the mysteries of the sexual nature of existence—biological and spiritual—are assigned to the given social structure. This structure is relative to historical changes. The modes of sexuality are subject to historical and sociological, and to legal and scientific, interpretation and prescription. The mythic and/or religious celebration of the mysteries of birth, life, and death is severely attenuated or disappears.

Once he began to glimpse the significance of the assimilation of sexuality—of, that is, the fundamental nature of the familial community—into the modern concept of history, Faulkner, we can conjecture with assurance, was compelled to the subject of his physical and spiritual inherence in history: to the substantive implication of his family in the history of Oxford, Lafayette County, the State of Mississippi, the South, the nation, and the world. He was seized by the modern "agenbite of inwit": the necessary experience of undefinable remorse the consciousness of the artist undergoes as a result of the historical displacement of the traditional community. An arrangement of human relations that seemed to embody both a natural and mystical permanence becomes the embodiment of a process of fundamental alteration. The community becomes the creature of history. Faulkner did not describe his experience of isolation in such weary academese. The experience came upon him in its typical attenuated American guise (the American settlement having been from the beginning an attenuation of the traditional community): a small town youth's sense of the evanescence of time and a nostalgia for the lost scene of boyhood; for, as Faulkner put it in the period when he first began to devote his writing to the world of his nativity, the "simple bread-and-salt of the world." But having become a writer he required more than a "touchstone" of the past. He must "recreate between the covers of a book the world I was already preparing to lose and regret." And the dimensions of this world —his own little postage stamp of a world—expanded prodigiously under the pressure of his genius as a literary artist once he commenced the sacramental act of preserving "my belief in the savor of the bread-and-salt." The act of memorial recreation became an act of historical creation. Faulkner's story of his world became, as the Bible is, an improvement on God, who, Faulkner observed in the exalted moment of his new-found vision, "dramatic though He be, has no sense, no feeling, for theatre."[16] Faulkner—like Balzac and Flaubert, Hawthorne and Melville, and not least Dickens—experienced the counterrevelation. This is to say a vision of the drama of modern man's comic, pathetic, and in moments, tragic inherence in history. So Faulkner joined the world historical poets.

But Faulkner's mind was too complex to subscribe easily to an imagination of historical process as man's fate. His identification with Pan, the cosmological poet, did not yield entirely—and would never do so—to an identification with the role of a purely world historical poet. The morphology of myth remains vivid in Faulkner's vision; it merely becomes recessive. It is fascinating to observe the ever growing complexity and sublety the cultural dialectic assumes in Faulkner's mind as it began to be embodied in the history of Yoknapatawpha County, even if the process can be detected only approximately.

When Faulkner began to conceive his vision of Yoknapataw-pha County, he appears to have made his first effort to get into focus in the story of Flem Snopes and the Frenchman Bend people a novelistic plan largely conforming to what Polonius would have called a "comical-pastoral-historical" story. "Father Abraham," as he called his uncompleted work, resembles George

Washington Harris' Sut Lovingood tales and Mark Twain's *Adventures of Huckleberry Finn*; both Harris and Mark Twain combine a pastoral sensibility (drawn ultimately, as all Western pastorals, from the classical paganism) with a strong feeling for historical realism. In Faulkner's case he was so conscious of his connection with Pan that, according to Blotner, he drew on the back of one page of the manuscript of "Father Abraham," evidently at the time he was writing the arresting fragment, a picture of himself as a faun, his back against a tree, piping the music for the dance of two fantastic creatures, half lamb and half rocking-horse.[17] He could have had in mind nothing more than the entertainment of a child, but the sketch may also be taken as a symbol of Faulkner's ironic concept of himself. Perhaps the amusing portrait of himself as a faun piping a dance for half real and half man-made creatures was a farewell to the role of the poet as a faun; or perhaps it was a recognition of the more subtle role the aspect of Pan would play in Faulkner's perception of the literary artist. Perhaps it intimates the demonic Pan who presides over various parts of the Snopes saga, his demonism having become a part of the historicity of sex rather than the sexuality of classical myth. Eventually, as we know, Flem Snopes becomes a figure of Satan, of Pan transformed at the moment of the Crucifixion. And all of the magnificent earthly fertility of Eula Varner is subjected to the constrictions of history. Even the most striking case of nympholepsy on record—that of Ike Snopes and the heifer—is reduced to the vulgar status of ordinary cow-diddling by the societal context in which it occurs.

When he left "Father Abraham" and turned his attention exclusively to the composition of *Flags in the Dust*, a story much closer to being for him a "touchstone of the past," Faulkner for the first time entered intimately into the historical perspective. In fact the subordination of the mythic frame of reference to a historical one in *Flags in the Dust* is, from the point of view of the argument I seek to develop, the notable feature of the first Yoknapatawpha novel. The historical perspective takes command; myth and tradition undergo the depredations of history.

The Sartorises exist in an aura of regret for the past; they live their lives in nostalgia—as though transplanted directly from medieval France into Mississippi—experiencing the intangible sense of a deprivation of the past known to historical societies but unknown in mythic and traditional ones. In *Flags in the Dust* the young Sartorises are destroyed trying to incorporate the airplane and the automobile, symbols of modern history, into their resistance to modernity. Byron Snopes prowls the community, writing his obscene love letters to Narcissa. The quality of Yoknapatawpha as a historic community—the condition of its historicity—is dramatically illustrated in the novel. But the teller of the tale in *Flags in the Dust* is an omniscient narrator, and Faulkner's sense of place in the story is objectively representational. For all the emphasis on history in the novel, the author tends to make myth and history parallel, to see somewhat as Eliot says Joyce does in *Ulysses*. Faulkner embodies his growing attraction to the historicity of existence in no character in the story. But moving from myth to mystery, his imagination was becoming more and more susceptible to the isolation of the individual by the modern historical process. He was more sensitive to the assertion of history against the individual and the attempted assertion of the individual against history.

Beginning more and more to experience the historicity of the modern storyteller, and to experience this in himself, Faulkner was ready to find his figure of the world historical poet—his Hamlet or Don Quixote, his Roderick Usher, his Ishmael.

Then he found Quentin Compson.

Of course he had probably known Quentin for some time before he found out his identity. If he ever truly found it out. Quentin may have been too close to him for the author's detached comprehension. I believe Louis D. Rubin, Jr., is surely right when he finds Joseph Blotner's biography to offer convincing confirmation of the personal affinity between Faulkner himself as a boy and youth and Quentin.[18]

So far as the employment of Quentin in the fiction is concerned, it seems likely that Quentin's role as the prophet and —shall we say?—the historian of the conscience and the consciousness of the Compsons had been glimpsed by Faulkner before he turned to *The Sound and the Fury*. Possibly too he had had intimations of the relationship between Quentin and his sister, having in fact anticipated this kind of relationship before, as in Josh and Pat in *Mosquitoes* and in Horace and Narcissa in *Flags in the Dust*. At any rate we know that Faulkner had it in mind to use Quentin as the teller of "Twilight," the contemplated story story from which *The Sound and the Fury* most immediately developed. Earlier he conceived the idea of using the Compson children as the source of at least part of the narration of a story about Nancy and Jesus. Joseph Blotner is inclined, moreover, to attribute the writing of the short story entitled "A Justice" to a period before the composition of *The Sound and the Fury*. In this story Quentin's role as narrator is definitely established. He is the twelve-year-old boy who recalls the story Sam Fathers tells him about the circumstances of his birth. In the conclusion of this story the scene is set for Quentin's future role as moral historian: Grandfather and the children get in the buggy to go back to town from the farm, and Quentin remarks that Caddy had "one fish, about the size of a chip, and she was wet to the waist." Then, Quentin says:

> We went on, in that strange, faintly sinister suspension of twilight in which I believed that I could still see Sam Fathers back there, sitting on his woodenblock, definite, immobile, and complete, like something looked upon after a long time in a preservation bath in a museum. That was it. I was just twelve then, and I would have to wait until I had passed on and through and beyond the suspension of twilight. Then I knew that I would know. But then Sam Fathers would be dead.[19]

Twenty-five years after he wrote *The Sound and the Fury*, Faulkner told Jean Stein, "Ishmael is the witness in *Moby Dick*, as I am Quentin in *The Sound and the Fury*."[20] I am not as inclined as some students of Faulkner to allow for the infallibility of his off-hand statements; in this case—I hope not simply because it suits my purpose to do so—I think Faulkner illuminates a concealment of the perspective in what may well be his greatest work—a work that may well be his greatest because of this concealment.

It is quite possible, I would agree, to think that Faulkner was confused in his remark. Did he actually mean to say," as I am Quentin in *Absalom, Absalom!*" This would seem to be more logical, for in this novel the central storytelling role of Quentin is patent. More than this, the overt presence of Quentin as a character is far more extensive; so it might seem that Faulkner's full interest in Quentin did not develop until the writing of the story about Sutpen. But the evidence indicates that the presentation of Quentin in *Absalom, Absalom!* is secondary to that in *The Sound and the Fury.* Quentin as he is at Harvard during the month before his suicide gains his authenticity from his large presence in *The Sound and the Fury.*

On the face of it such an emphasis on Quentin appears to contradict the well-known four-fold perspective of *The Sound and the Fury.* The first three sections are told by Benjy, Quentin, and Jason, respectively, the last by an omniscient narrator. But where is the informing consciousness pervading *The Sound and the Fury?* And where does it derive from? Who is the truly responsive witness to the scene when Caddy in her muddy drawers climbed the tree to look in on the mourning for Damuddy? It is not the mindless Benjy nor the rationalist Jason; but Quentin, who had told Caddy to take off her dress and had splashed water on her so that she slipped and fell down in the stream and got mud on her drawers. It is the virginal Quentin who conceives an incestuous love for Caddy, not because he would ever actually commit incest, but because through "some presbyterian concept of its eternal punishment" he could "cast himself and his sister both into hell . . . where he could guard her forever and keep her forevermore intact amid the eternal fires," and so escape forever from the burden of history.[21] In Quentin's relationship with Caddy, the theme of the historicity of sexual motivation—of the response of sexuality to the forces of history —is symbolized more powerfully than it is in "The Fall of the House of Usher," *Pierre,* or *The Turn of the Screw,* as powerfully as in *Madame Bovary*. But what is still more powerful, I think, is the implication the theme develops in Quentin's agonized interior monologue. I mean the historicism of consciousness. I mean the implication in *The Sound and the Fury* of how in the modern world, bereft of mythic and traditional order save as this appears in the trappings of nostalgia, the "dark, harsh flowing of time" is channeled directly into the sensitive self instead of the family and the community. In these cold waters Quentin strives for a purchase on the symbols of order; carrying on his crazed struggle to save the "frail doomed vessel" of his "family's honor," he transforms honor into doom—willfully yielding the vain myth of himself as a savior to implacable historical imperatives. I mean, too, the way Caddy (according to that prose poem, the Compson genealogy, which Faulkner wrote fifteen years after *The Sound and the Fury*) in her inextricable attachment to Quentin lives out his love of death—his impotence, his incapacity to love, his isolation. She names her half-anonymous bastard child after him because the child is truly Quentin's heir—the girl Quentin who disappears out of a window with the money she stole from Jason (though it was rightfully hers) and is never seen or reported upon again. But Caddy, whom Faulkner says he loved passionately, had to be reported upon again. And she is. She is a creased and recreased photograph from a glossy picture magazine folded in the hand of the shocked, mousy librarian Melissa Meek. In the photograph sitting beside a middle-aged Nazi staff general in a chromium Mercedes is Caddy, still beautiful, and serene in her damnation. A figure in the obscene Nazi historical perversion of a pagan and mythic society, Caddy disappears in the unspeakable Götterdämmerung of a modern paganism.Caddy knows her doom, knows it and accepts it, understanding somehow her role in Quentin's struggle with history. Understanding that if to Benjy she was partly a mother, partly a nymph of water and trees, and to Jason a worthless bitch, she was to Quentin a symbol of his resistance to history and that being so she was caught up in the remorseful, murky historicism of her brother's consciousness of time, sex, death, and damnation. Caught up, we might say, in the power of the God of John Knox, which Quentin had in his puritan desperation ruthlessly arrogated to himself. If it is true—poetically speaking—that Faulkner wrote the first three sections of *The Sound and the Fury* under the impress of a witness like Quentin Compson, no dying god but a world historical neurotic and self-defeated historian, it helps to explain, I think, why in writing the Benjy section he had felt, as he was to say later, an "ecstasy and also a bafflement." He had experienced a transcendent fulfillment of his long novitiate in the literary priesthood, the ineffable joy of the self-certification of his creativity. And yet he had too experienced when he had finished the section a feeling of being enclosed in a perfected work of art, as though he had sealed himself in that same Byzantine vase the Reverend Mr. Mahon refers to in *Soldiers' Pay*. Faulkner says that he wrote Quentin's and Jason's sections trying to clarify Benjy's. But he knew that he had not written three discrete interior monologues. In the tortured account of the familial relationships of the Compsons as told by each of the three narrators he had dramatized the imprisonment of sexuality in history. Still, he had made the inner truth of the modern writer's consciousness of existence—that is, to say, his awareness of its subjection to historicity, as symbolized most prominently in the novel by Quentin's and Caddy's incestuous connection—the theme of Benjy's and Jason's sections no less than of Quentin's. He had identified the consciousness of each narrator with the historicity of the literary artist as he had found this in Quentin.

This is an insight Faulkner glimpses I think in a curious depiction of the Southern literary artist in a preface to *The Sound and the Fury* that he set down in 1933, five years after the writing of the novel, but never published. (This and another version of the unpublished preface have recently been brought out by Mr. Meriwether, one in *The Southern Review* and one in *The Mississippi Quarterly*. I refer to the latter here.) Faulkner states—although in what he evidently thought of as a kind of prose poem and thus in condensed, somewhat enigmatic language —that the person who elects to be an artist in the South does so on his own because the South has no art, having been dead since the Civil War. The choice involves the Southern writer in violence. Once it might have been physical; Southern writers were given to horsewhipping or shooting editors who maltreated their manuscripts. But now the violence is psychic. Since the Southern writer is isolated from his environment, leaving him with only himself to write about, he has to make the necessary connection with his world, although it is dead and lacks even the sense of artistic tradition available in Chicago. He must join his self-created will to art to what history has made of the South: "Because it is himself that the Southerner is writing about, not about his environment: who has, figuratively speaking, taken the artist in him in one hand and his milieu in the other and thrust the one into the other like a clawing and spitting cat into a croaker sack. And he writes."

> We seem to try in the simple furious breathing (or writing) span of the individual to draw a savage indictment of the contemporary scene or to escape from it into a make believe region of swords and magnolias and mockingbirds which perhaps never existed anywhere. . . . Each course is a matter of violent partizanship, in which the writer unconsciously writes into every line and phrase his violent despairs and rages and frustrations or his violent prophesies and still more violent hopes. That cold intellect which can write with complete detachment and gusto of its contemporary scene is not among us.[22]

But in *The Sound and the Fury*, Faulkner says, he can see after five years that he tried both to indict and to escape the South at one time. What he means is that he had put art and artist integrally into the story—that is, without the awareness of thrusting the first into the second by main force. He had entered into the depths of meaning he articulated fully only once —this later on (and with the climactic simplicity of a truth revealed) in *Absalom, Absalom!*, when in the "iron New England dark," Quentin says of the South, "I don't hate it."

Once he looked through Quentin's eyes at Sam Fathers distanced in the mythic twilight and moved with Quentin's mind toward the day when he would pass from the ahistorical childhood vision of the old people into the knowledge of modernity, Faulkner discovered in Quentin the first profound portrayal of his own imagination—a fiction yet a symbol of a deep inner reality, a powerful apprehension of modern existence. (And besides that, it may be that Faulkner discovered a symbolic brother who assumed one of Faulkner's deepest longings, the desire for a sister.) Through Quentin, Faulkner could pass beyond the attachment to myth, tradition, or revelation; beyond the vision of the cyclical pattern of existence, or of the pattern in the climactic events of Christian history: the Nativity, Crucifixion, and Resurrection. He could experience how, these possible faiths failing, the consciousness knows only a relentless and an entire inherence of body and spirit in the historical process.

Faulkner was never truly to transcend his identification of the imagination of the literary artist with the compelling historicism of the modern consciousness of existence. Even though he repeatedly rebelled against it: a few times in some of his greatest rhetoric, as in the Nobel Prize speech; and no doubt also, at great length, in the much abused non-Yoknapatawpha novel *A Fable*. His first, and most powerful, rebellion occurred in *The Sound and the Fury* itself, when in the last section he attempted "to get completely out the book," this essentially by employing an omniscient narrator to give the testimony of two interrelated witnesses to the actuality of the Christian historical revelation. One of these is Dilsey. The more basic witness is the Negro preacher, the Reverend Shegog. A visitor in the pulpit of the little church Dilsey attends, he preaches the Easter sermon on the day after Caddy's daughter has run away and while Jason is pursuing her. A visitor to Jefferson from St. Louis, he is a highly educated and sophisticated man, although he is little and looks like a monkey. But the outstanding feature of this St. Louis preacher is his dual nature. He is actually two men. In one guise the Reverend Shegog sounds "like a white man" as (controlled and poised like a man on a tight rope) he delivers a carefully phrased message in a cold, level, educated, rational voice. But then he pauses and in a tone utterly different announces, "Breddren and sistuhn, I got de ricklickshun en de blood of the

Lamb!" In the moments that follow he becomes a literal believer; his words become incarnate in his body and he is transformed into "a serene, tortured crucifix."[23] And Christ is present in the little Negro church. But at no altar, in no miracle of transubstantiation. Christ is present in the historical moment: a witness to His own Crucifixion and to His own Resurrection as historical facts. "There is only one relation to revealed truth," Kierkegaard said, "believing it." The realization of the Kingdom of God in the fullness of time as assured by a conviction of the historical events surrounding God's incarnation in man—this concept of history is reaffirmed in Dilsey's church on Easter Sunday, April 8, 1928, in Jefferson, Yoknapatawpha County, Mississippi. Dilsey is witness to the reaffirmation. And in the simple but profound vision that comes to her during the Easter Service, the destiny of the Compsons is embodied in the historicity of revealed truth: "I've seed de first en de last."

But at the end of the fourth section of *The Sound and the Fury*, Quentin's witness returns. In the ironic moment when Luster swings the buggy to the left instead of to the accustomed right of the Confederate memorial on the square and all the order of Benjy's world is suddenly destroyed, Quentin—though he had been dead for eighteen years and though he was already a ghost when he drowned himself in the Charles River, Cambridge, Massachusetts, June, 2, 1910—is once again fully present in the story, the dark consciousness of a South still living its death in history.

It has been kept in mind, I trust, that in remarking upon Faulkner and the legend of the artist I have been speaking about the artist in the modern age. The term modern is still a convenient one to use, but, as we all know, the modern age has by now ceased to be. In the modern age the mythic and the traditional were replaced by history. In the age now beginning history is probably to be replaced by something else. What this may be we of course do not know.

Life is a tale "Told by an idiot, full of sound and fury,/ Signifying nothing." This statement of futility by Macbeth—together with Hamlet's soliloquy: "To be or not to be . . ."—is the first formulation of what I have awkwardly termed the historicism of consciousness. Shakespeare experienced in his imagination of Hamlet and Macbeth the imposition of the burden of history that the consciousness had to assume with the depletion of the life of the consciousness incorporated in myth and in traditionalism. By its very nature this is not a theme that can be inherited by one generation after another. In one way or another it has been discovered in each generation of literary artists since Shakespeare, the discoveries growing more poignant as the sense of the mythic and the traditional have become more and more marginal in the consciousness. One of the most poignant experiences of the impingement of history upon the fading margins of myth and tradition occurred in the literary imagination of the post-World War I American South. Quentin Compson is the preeminent legend of this imagination. He knew what Hamlet and Macbeth knew, and Caddy, out of her love for her loveless brother, shared what he knew with him. And Faulkner—who created the brother and sister and who ruthlessly imagined their terrible images of the world—shared what they knew with them. He knew what he was saying when he said, "as I am Quentin in *The Sound and the Fury.*"

NOTES

1. "Voyage with Don Quixote," *Essays by Thomas Mann* (New York: Vintage Books, 1957), pp. 325–69.

2. *The Enlightenment: An Interpretation. The Rise of Modern Paganism* (New York: Vintage Books, 1968), p. xi.

3. Joseph Blotner, *Faulkner: A Biography* (New York: Random House, 1974), I, p. 422.

4. *Pan the Goat-God: His Myth in Modern Times* (Cambridge, Mass.: Harvard University Press, 1969).

5. See ibid., pp. 1–16 for a discussion of the origins of the Pan myth; pp. 77–133 for a discussion of Pan in mid nineteenth-century writings. The translation of Gautier's poem is on p. 107; Browning's poem is quoted on p. 86.

6. See ibid., illustration No. 15, following p. 144. Also, see pp. 195–219.

7. *The Marble Faun and a Green Bough* (New York: Random House, n.d.). Photographic reproduction of the two volumes, originally published 1924, 1933 respectively. Quotations from *The Marble Faun,* pp. 12, 16, 46.

8. See Noel Polk, "William Faulkner's *Marionettes,*" *Mississippi Quarterly,* 26 (Summer 1973), pp. 247–80.

9. "Nympholepsy," ed. James B. Meriwether, *Mississippi Quarterly,* 26 (Summer 1973), pp. 403–09.

10. "Out of Nazareth," *New Orleans Sketches,* ed. Carvel Collins (New Brunswick, N.J. Rutgers University Press, 1958), pp. 102, 104, 110.

11. *Collected Stories of William Faulkner* (New York: Random House, 1950), p. 805. The entire story occupies pp. 799–821.

12. Ibid., p. 899. "Carcassonne" is to be found on pp. 895–900.

13. *Soldiers' Pay* (New York: Liveright Publishing Corporation, 1954), pp. 61, 297, 319.

14. William Faulkner, *Mosquitoes* (New York: Dell Publishing Company, 1962), pp. 119–20, 40, 266–70, 277–81.

15. Ibid., 202–09; *New Orleans Sketches,* ed. Collins, p. 38.

16. Blotner, *Faulkner,* pp. 531–32.

17. Ibid., pp. 529–31.

18. See Rubin's review of Blotner's *Faulkner, Chronicle of Higher Education,* 8, No. 25 (March 25, 1974), pp. 11–12.

19. "A Justice," *Collected Stories,* p. 360.

20. Blotner, *Faulkner,* II, 1522.

21. *The Sound and the Fury* (New York: The Modern Library, 1956), p. 411.

22. "An Introduction to *The Sound and the Fury,*" ed. James B. Meriwether, *Mississippi Quarterly,* 26 (Summer 1973), 412.

23. *The Sound and the Fury,* pp. 336–38.

# *five*   Sally R. Page

# *Faulkner's Sense of the Sacred*

The central motif of modern literature and life has been despair.
Fragmentation, alienation, and dehumanization have plagued
modern man who has lost his primitive sense of belonging to a
creative natural order because he views existence as chaos rather
than cosmos. There is no set of universal values, no reliable code
to live by which will assure a meaningful life experience. In his
*Toward a Psychology of Being* Abraham Maslow says,

> The state of being without a system of values is psycho-
> pathogenic. . . . The human being needs a framework of values,
> a philosophy of life, a religion or religion-surrogate to live by
> and understand by, in about the same sense that he needs sun-
> light, calcium or love. . . . Historically, we are in a value
> interregnum in which all externally given value systems have
> proven to be failures, e.g., nothing is worth dying for. . . .[1]

In *Religions, Values and Peak Experiences* Maslow laments that
"most humanistic scholars and artists have shared in the general
collapse of all traditional values." They are "disheartened or pessi-
mistic or despairing, and a fair portion are nihilistic or cynical (in
the sense of believing that no 'good life' is possible . . .). And
[Maslow goes on to ask] which well-known artists or writers
today are trying to teach, to inspire, to conduce to virtue? Which
of them could even use this word 'virtue' without gagging? Upon
which of them can an 'idealistic' young man model himself."[2] The
fiction of William Faulkner, despite its portrayal of man's alienation and despair is, of course, a notable exception to Maslow's

description of modern literature. It is, instead, I believe, prophetic of a new age of hopefulness about the possibilities of human life and of assurance about what is significant, meaningful, and valuable to human living.

Contemporary theologians, philosophers, and humanistic psychologists like Maslow are struggling to discover a "validated, usable system of human values that we can believe in and devote ourselves to (be willing to die for), because they are true rather than because we are exhorted to 'believe and have faith.' "[3] The search for values has turned man to himself. "There's no place else to turn but inward, to the self, as the locus of values."[4] Turning inward to self means the possibility of the discovery of the full potential of what it means to be human. It is Faulkner's sense of the sacredness and the potential wholeness of the human being that makes his fiction an invaluable resource in the contemporary quest for the rediscovery of the essential truths of life.

The question of the nature of the self and the parallel question of the nature of human existence are the most important issues which face modern man. Maslow says that the most important contribution of existentialist philosophy to modern psychology is its "radical stress on the concept of identity and the experience of identity as a *sine qua non* of human nature and of any philosophy or science of human nature."[5] "Existentialism rests on phenomenology, i.e., it uses personal, subjective experience as the foundation upon which abstract knowledge is built." The stress is on "starting from experiential knowledge rather than from systems of concepts or abstract categories or a prioris."[6] Faulkner's fiction is grounded in the portrayal of protagonists who are struggling through critical identity experiences—characters such as Horace Benbow, Quentin Compson, Joe Christmas, Addie Bundren, and Thomas Sutpen. Furthermore, the very nature of fiction—and especially is this true of Faulkner's fiction—means a focus on personal experience, that is, the interaction of the inner man, the unconscious, instinctual, intuitive and conscious self, with the world. Fiction is an excellent vehicle for exploring and embodying the experience of human identity because it captures and preserves more effectively than can any theology, philosophy, or psychology the sense of what it means to be alive as a human being.[7]

The crucial identity question facing modern man is what it means to be a whole person, to be an integrated human being, and, also, what it means "to know" in a holistic way. It is only out of self-knowledge and wholeness that a "validated," "usable," and "true" system of values can come. The power and emotional forcefulness of Faulkner's fiction stem from his focus on the crucial issues of Being, Knowing, and Valuing. Faulkner's fiction demonstrates that if we are to discover and to experience wholeness, we must become aware of and integrate into consciousness powerful forces of the unconscious self, which is not simply a reservoir of destructiveness and primitive fears but which is more basically a resource of "potentialities of the greatest dynamism,"[8] of "joy, love, creativeness, play and humor...."[9]

> With the dawn of consciousness the world became ambivalent, sundered into opposites by cognition, which opened up a deep chasm between spontaneity and reflection. Ego-consciousness brought with it a sense of loneliness, its genesis being experienced as guilt and suffering, as inevitable punishment.... The human psyche, as the source of all religious and cultural phenomena, stores the knowledge man had accumulated before the advent of self-awareness. To establish the link with this buried treasure through the aid of his conscious mind, to realize the images dormant in his psyche, has become a cultural necessity if man is to regain wholeness.[10]

Faulkner's fiction helps us recover those necessary images that lie dormant in the human psyche, for its major theme is the exploration of those unconscious forces that drive human beings to be, to know, and to act. Faulkner's vision of hope for human life rests on his understanding of the unconscious self as a powerful and dynamic resource of life, wholeness, and essential human values. Faulkner's fiction shows that through an awareness of his deepest self, man can experience a sense of oneness with the natural flow of life and can recapture the sense of the sacred dimension of human being.

The motivating force behind Faulkner's fiction as well as the motivating force in his most dynamic characters is the urge toward wholeness. Faulkner viewed this urge as the most basic drive in human life; it is experienced as a deep, inner yearning for love, for understanding, for satisfaction, for fulfillment, and completeness. The continual struggle to satisfy that yearning propels the individual forward through the growth process. Faulkner's fiction suggests that there are crucial events in the growth cycle when the experience of wholeness is available in a powerful way, and that if the individual is unable to achieve that experience of wholeness and satisfaction when he is intensely aware of his need of it, he will experience an extreme sense of alienation from life. On the other hand, if the individual is able to experience a sense of wholeness, to integrate into his consciousness and life experience his inner drive for growth, creativity, love, and unity, he will experience transcendence, tranquility, and inner serenity.

The drive for wholeness, for union, for a sense of oneness, is so powerful, Faulkner suggests, that if it is impossible for the character to experience it in life, he will be driven to death as a means of satisfying his yearning. However, if the character is able to find satisfaction in the natural processes of life and in the growth cycle, he will continue his journey through life with an attitude of hope and delight, a delight that springs not only from his joy in the pleasures of life but also from an essential optimism about the nature of human existence. Faulkner's vision of life is one of hope because it assures us that in the end the struggle of life will be satsifying.

The movement of Faulkner's fiction, viewed as a whole, is from yearning and desire through struggle, suffering, and death to birth and delight—a cycle that is a pattern of growth which is basic to the very structure of life.

Faulkner's early fiction focuses on yearning and desire. As I have shown in *Faulkner's Women*, the motivating force behind Faulkner's early works is a powerful, driving urge, a yearning for fulfillment and satisfaction. The desire is manifested primarily in terms of a yearning for sexual fulfillment. Nearly all of the early poems focus on intense romantic love, and the images that portray the lover's yearning express the need to reach outside the self and the present moment to an idealized past or else to the realm of the stars. This same kind of yearning is expressed in *The Marble Faun* as a desire to return to a natural world that is portrayed as the Golden Age, a Paradise, in which the natural flow of life is creative, loving, free, and satisfying. It is the marble faun's vision of the potential of life that is embodied in the natural process that makes his sense of frustration and alienation particularly acute. Transcendence through nature is the subject of the short sketch, "The Hill," in which the protagonist experiences a fleeting moment of satisfaction that enables him to face the dull routine of his life with greater strength.

> Here, in the dusk, nymphs and fauns might riot to a shrilling of thin pipes, to a shivering and hissing of cymbals in a sharp volcanic abasement beneath a tall icy star. Behind him was the motionless conflagration of sunset, before him was the opposite valley rim upon the changing sky. For a while he stood on one horizon and stared across at the other, far above a world of endless toil and troubled slumber; untouched, untouchable; forgetting, for a space, that he must return.[11]

These heightened, ecstatic accounts of the experience of transcendence through romantic love and through nature are occasions when the potential for love, creativity, growth, and wholeness emerges from the unconscious self into consciousness.[12] Maslow's psychology of the healthy, growing person suggests that the personality is a combination of the past, the actualities of the present, and the potentialities of the future. Growth needs and future potential are alive in the present state of being of the person in the form of goals, hopes, wishes, desires, fantasies, and imaginings.[13] Every satisfaction of a growth need leads to the emergence of a higher need so that human growth is an ever upward spiral, a continuing struggle toward completion and wholeness. This spiral growth upward is experienced psychically when the forces of life—love, creativity, sexuality, and potential being—emerge from the unconscious into consciousness. Maslow has identified this psychic occurrence as a peak experience, an occasion when there is a momentary sense of wholeness that anticipates the full potential of the human being.[14] Maslow suggests that such peak experiences are necessary steps in the process of growth, the process of uncovering, discovering, and creating the essential Being of the individual. This type of "cognitive happening" has been identified by Maslow as a fairly frequent occurrence in "the B-love experience, the parental experience, the mystic, or oceanic, or nature experience, the aesthetic perception, the creative moment, the therapeutic or intellectual insight, the orgasmic experience, and certain forms of athletic fulfillment."[15] The peak experience provides a model for an understanding of integration and wholeness and of the holistic way of knowing.

Both *Soldiers' Pay* and *Mosquitoes* are climaxed by peak experiences in which the narrators find momentarily the satisfaction that they have sought through sexuality in visions of wholeness, unity, and transcendence. Images of golden beauty, flight, a swirling upward, of coherence and union characterize the two passages. At the end of *Soldiers' Pay* Faulkner describes the singing of a Negro choir:

> It was nothing, it was everything; . . . Feed thy Sheep, O Jesus. All the longing of mankind for a Oneness with something, somewhere. . . . no organ was needed as above the harmonic passion of bass and baritone soared a clear soprano of women's voices like a flight of gold and heavenly birds. (*SP*, p. 319)

The vision that concludes *Mosquitoes* of the "headless, armless, legless torso of a girl, motionless and virginal and passionately eternal before the shadows and echoes whirl away" is a similar peak experience that captures the sense of wholeness and satisfaction in an aesthetic experience that is described as a dream-like state of mind outside of normal time and space. Fairchild's definition of artistic genius also expresses the sense of wholeness that is characteristic of the peak experience.

> It is that Passion Week of the heart . . . that passive state of the heart with which the mind, the brain has nothing to do at all, in which the hackneyed accidents which make up this world—love

and life and sex and sorrow—brought together by chance in perfect proportions, take on a kind of splendid and timeless beauty. (*M*, p. 339)

The powerful images and experiences that Faulkner focuses on at climactic points in his early works—the lure of sex and of woman's beauty, romantic love, the natural world portrayed as a Golden Age, the images of spring, of sunlight and rustling leaves, of flight, of a rising upward, of the perfection and wholeness of art, and of the longing for "Oneness with something, somewhere"—are all expressions of the same basic urge, an unconscious drive that can be defined as the life force, the urge to grow and to reach beyond a present state of being to the fulfillment of the potential that is present and alive in the personality and is expressed in terms of a yearning for the ultimate goal of growth —wholeness of the self and a sense of Oneness with the Universe or with God.

One of the most interesting of Faulkner's descriptions of a peak experience is found in the short story "Carcassonne":

> ". . . me on a buckskin pony with eyes like blue electricity and a mane like tangled fire, galloping up the hill right off into the high heaven of the world. . . . Steed and rider thunder on, thunder punily diminishing; a dying star upon the immensity of darkness and of silence within which steadfast, fading, deep-breasted and grave of flank, muses the dark and tragic figure of the Earth, his mother." (*CS*, p. 900)

Originally, I interpreted this passage as an indication that Faulkner's realization of the fading of the ideal made him turn away from romantic idealism and turn instead to the Earth—to the world of actuality. Certainly, Faulkner did see the inadequacy of "living in the stars," of attempting to sustain permanently any idealized peak experience, or of expecting to find in real life the actualization of his vision in the same terms and with the same intensity with which it could be experienced in the imagination. However, I see now that what Faulkner's fiction suggests is not that idealism and the desire for transcendence should be abandoned, but that they should be integrated into the life experience. Apart from the world of reality, romantic idealism (which is the idealization of the life force) diminishes and eventually evaporates; on the other hand, the life that does not integrate ideals, fantasies, and dreams into the actualities of existence ends in disillusionment and despair.

The powerful fiction of the middle phase of Faulkner's career —from *The Sound and the Fury* to *The Wild Palms*—focuses on the struggle and suffering of protagonists who are unable to realize their driving urge for the achievement of love, creativity, union, and wholeness in their actual life experiences. Faulkner's powerfully rendered tragic figures—Quentin Compson, Joe Christmas, Gail Hightower, Addie Bundren, Thomas Sutpen, and Charlotte Rittenmeyer—are seriously involved in the search for wholeness of Being. They possess an intense, heightened awareness of their inner selves, and they are extremely conscious of their alienation from the life process. However, they are locked into a static emotional state in which growth cannot take place because they are unable to integrate the life force into their lives and, therefore, to experience satisfaction and fulfillment. Faulkner portrays them in the critical moments of an identity crisis in which the yearning for the satisfaction of the drives within them has reached such a heightened level of emotional intensity that climax and resolution are inevitable.

All of the images that dominate Faulkner's portrayal of Quentin Compson's last day of life in *The Sound and the Fury* are the outward manifestations in the natural world of the powerful psychic images of the life force that is struggling to emerge from his unconscious self. The sun, the flowers, the water, the trout rising in the stream beneath the glistening sunlight, the cool groves of trees, the child, the bread, the lush blossoms of the trees, the season itself, the motionless gull high above the glinting water—all of nature blends with the life force that is available within Quentin as a resource for growth. However, Quentin represses the powerful urge for life, for love, and for union because he can understand his needs only in terms of his possessive love for his sister. "If it could just be a hell beyond that: the clean flame the two of us more than dead. Then you will have only me then only me then the two of us amid the pointing and the horror beyond the clean flame" (*S&F*, p. 144). In order to move from desiring to possess an idealized virgin Caddy to experiencing an unneeding, creative love for his sister, Quentin would have to come to terms with his own sexuality in a way that he is unable to do. He cannot accept the reality of his sexual desire for his sister and move beyond desire to love; the result is that the growth process is brought to a standstill in Quentin. He envisions transcendence and union not in terms of love and creativity but in terms of death and complete possessiveness.

Gail Hightower's idealization of his ancestor storming into Jefferson on his stallion is much like Quentin's idealization of Caddy's virginity. It represents the vision of glory, power, exhiliration, and transcendence—of life power—that Hightower needs to integrate into his experience. Instead, however, his mind focuses only on his ideal, while his wife, with whom he has been unable to share either love or sexual fulfillment, commits suicide in a Memphis brothel. Like Quentin, Hightower is caught in a psychic stasis—he is unable to move emotionally; he is unable to grow and to experience love. However, in the last passages of *Light in August* Hightower experiences an identity crisis that moves him toward self-realization.

Faulkner captures Quentin's inward struggle to search out the maze of his unconscious self, his past, his feelings, and his desires by dramatizing the struggle in terms of wandering. In a trance, a dreamlike state of mind, Quentin wanders through the countryside searching for his deepest self. In a similar, trancelike state of mind, Hightower explores his deepest, inward self. His mental journey is described as a turning wheel of faces, and as his past, his feelings, his desires, and his actions parade before him, he experiences a powerful awareness of their real meaning. He is able to come to terms with who he has been—to see that the vision of "the single instant in which a horse galloped and a gun crashed" has been the "debaucher and murderer" of his wife (*LA*, p. 430).

It is significant that Hightower's inward journey of self-discovery is triggered by a peak experience of peace and momentary transcendence that occurs immediately after he has assisted Lena Grove in giving birth to her son. Walking through the woods he feels

> the intermittent sun, the heat, smelling the savage and fecund odor of the earth, the woods, the loud silence. "I should never have lost this habit, too. But perhaps they will both come back to me, if this itself be not the same as prayer." (*LA*, p. 356)

The experience with birth and with nature and the thought of prayer enable Hightower to see a vision of regeneration. As the charred planks of the plantation home of the barren Joanna Burden loom before him, he is able to envision the "rich fecund black life of the quarters, the mellow shouts, the presence of fecund women, the prolific naked children in the dust before the doors; and the big house again, noisy, loud with the treble shouts of the generations" (*LA*, p. 357). Although he experiences self-discovery, Hightower is unable to incorporate the power of regeneration into his own life.

The identity crisis that Joe Christmas experiences in *Light in August* also represents a failure to incorporate satisfactorily the potentials of the life force into the actual life experience. Joe Christmas is caught in a circle of lovelessness, dehumanization, and emotional stasis which he is unable to break out of until the last few days of his life. His entire life experience is characterized by actions that represent a perverse devaluing of the forces of life and of love. Christmas's birth takes place under the shadow of a grandfather who allows his daughter to die in childbirth and who intentionally seeks to destroy her son. Christmas's first encounter with sexuality, when he accidentally sees the dietitian with the doctor, is an experience that focuses on shame, dishonesty, punishment, and confusion. His foster father can express caring only in terms of violence and coercion, and Joe is brutally betrayed by his lover, the only person with whom he was ever able to experience openness and trust. Therefore, all the forces that draw Christmas toward life are violently rejected, for his past experience prevents him from trusting life. He refuses the food that Mrs. McEachern and Joanna Burden prepare for him; he resists the powerful, drawing images of the life force that emerge from the natural world; and he rejects the Negro world, which could give him a sense of belonging and which Faulkner portrays as rich with the forces of life. Though he is sexually active, his sexuality is an expression of anger, hatred, violence, and alienation rather than of love, creativity, and union.

As with Quentin and Hightower, Christmas's struggle for wholeness reaches a crisis of intensity that is portrayed in terms of a trance or dreamlike state in which there is a loss of consciousness of place or of the passage of time. Christmas's outward journey during the last few days of his life is symbolic of his inward journey into his unconscious self. Gradually, he begins to experience a sense of oneness with nature; he wants to know the time, and he wants food. However, as he at last gives himself up to his fate—his acceptance of his identity as Negro—"the black shoes smelling of Negro" that he has put on his feet become "the gauge definite and ineradicable of the black tide creeping up his legs, moving from his feet upward as death moves" (*LA*, p. 297).

It is significant that all three of these characters who struggle seriously and intensely with their inner selves and the problem of personal identity experience a resolution that is characterized either by a sense of peace or a sense of psychic uplifting. Quentin's life ends with death by water, a symbol not only of death but also of regeneration. For Quentin "to not be" is "peace"— hardly a healthy realization of the drives within him but, nevertheless, a release of tension that gives him relief from the struggle. Faulkner suggests that Hightower's ability to be honest with himself, to recognize his destructiveness, and to accept responsibility for his life frees him at his death from the emotional stasis that has controlled his existence. The galloping horses at last rush past and are gone; all that remains of the vision is the "dust swirling skyward" and fading into the night and the faint sound in the distance of "clashing sabres" and "thundering hooves." Such images suggest that death is experienced as a transformation which brings peace and freedom. Joe Christmas's death is a transcendent or peak experience, apparently not only for himself but for those who witness it, in which the experience of the loss of consciousness at death is portrayed as a peaceful swirling upward into the stars. Percy Grimm's castration of Christmas is the horrible symbolic enactment of how the South's hatred of the Negro has destroyed the potential of the life force in him. Faulkner's description of Joe's death, however, affirms the power of the force of life to overcome the power of death:

> For a long moment he looked up at them with peaceful and unfathomable and unbearable eyes. Then his face, body, all seemed to collapse, to fall in upon itself, and from out the slashed garments about his hips and loins the pent black blood seemed to rush like a released breath. It seemed to rush out of his pale body like the rush of sparks from a rising rocket; upon that black blast the man seemed to rise soaring into their memories forever and ever. (*LA*, p. 407)

It is significant that these characters do not just die; instead, Faulkner suggests that at death they are embraced by a loving Universe which fulfills the need that has driven them throughout their lives, the yearning for transcendence and for a peaceful merger with the unity of creation. In *The Mansion* Mink, who has dedicated his life to affirming his own value as a human being by avenging his betrayal by Flem, experiences this same kind of death. As Mink feels himself sinking into the ground he knows that death leaves folks

> all mixed and jumbled up comfortable and easy so wouldn't nobody even know or even care who was which any more, himself among them, equal to any, good as any, brave as any, being inextricable from, anonymous with all of them: the beautiful, the splendid, the proud and the brave, right on up to the very top itself among the shining phantoms and dreams which are the milestones of the long human recordings—Helen and the bishops, the kings and the unhomed angels, the scornful and graceless seraphim. (*M*, p. 436)

In all of the fiction of the middle phase of Faulkner's career there is a great emphasis on the need of the characters to establish their sexual identity. Just as in the early works, these tragic figures struggle to experience satisfaction and wholeness through sexuality. Faulkner's fiction is a powerful portrayal of the intimate connection between the experience of personal identity and self-knowledge and the experience of sexual identity. The pattern of sexual encounter—desire, involvement, climax, and withdrawal—is the structural pattern of initiation and of self-discovery. It embodies the archetypal psychological pattern of any experience of intimate knowing of self, of others, or of the essential truths of life. Much of the emotional forcefulness of Faulkner's fiction lies in his willingness to deal with human sexuality in an open and intimate way and to explore its role in the growth process.

Faulkner's fiction demonstrates again and again that intimate sexual relationships, both family relationships and male-female relationships, are a major force in the formation of identity. The character's attitude toward sexual encounter is a reflection of his self-image, which in turn determines his attitude toward the nature of human existence. Consider, for example, Quentin's suicidal need to possess his sister sexually, Christmas's physical illness when he learns about menstruation and his murder of his sexual partner, Addie Bundren's violent whipping of the school children to relieve her aloneness, and Charlotte Rittenmeyer's suicidal determination to have an abortion *in contrast to* Lena Grove's amused acceptance of her sexuality as she climbs out of the window to leave home and search for her lover, the pregnant woman's trust of the flow of life in "Old Man," Emmy's sense of the sacredness of her sexual encounter with Donald in *Soldiers' Pay*, and Eula Snopes's dignified acceptance of the power of sexual attraction: "You just are, and you need, and you must, and so you do" (*T*, p. 94).

Sexuality is a powerful means of releasing the dynamic forces of the unconscious self. However, sexuality is a life force only when it is integrated with the healthy powers of the unconscious self—love, creativity, growth, unity, and potential Being. Sexuality can be a powerful force of regeneration if it is accepted and integrated by the experience of self-giving love; if it is repressed, devalued, or used to express feelings of anger, hatred, or violence, it can be meaningless, perverse, alienating, dehumanizing, and destructive.

A reaction to sexuality of shame, shock, fear, violence, repression, possessiveness, or rejection is destructive of self and of life; on the other hand, a reaction to sexuality that reflects an integration of sexuality with the dynamic qualities of the life force—joy, love, creativeness, play, humor, and unity—is life-nourishing and life-sustaining. [I am quoting again from Maslow.] "On the whole, most philosophies and religions, Eastern as well as Western, have dichotomized" the "twofold nature of man, his lower and his higher, his creatureliness and his god-likeness . . . teaching that the way to become 'higher' is to renounce and master the 'lower.' The existentialists, however, teach that *both* are simultaneously defining characteristics of human nature. Neither can be repudiated; they can only be integrated."[16] The alienation and frustration that have dominated modern life are the result of the emphasis of the modern age on the split between the physical world and the world of the spirit. Faulkner's fiction reflects his intense awareness of this split and his sense of the need of modern man to bridge the chasm. His fiction is a witness to the human need for experiencing sexuality—and life—not out of a fragmented, dehumanized, or destructive sense of self but out of self-acceptance, wholeness, and a sense of openness and trust.

The relationship of Donald and Emmy in *Soldiers' Pay* is an example of Faulkner's sense of the potential sacredness of sexuality. Faulkner's description of their sexual encounter captures all those psychic images that embody man's sense of peace, serenity, love, and oneness with nature and with the natural process that are available to him from the resources of his unconscious self. Emmy is able to give herself to Donald freely and spontaneously out of a deep sense of openness and trust. The temporary merger of her identity with his enlarges her as a person, and she is deeply aware of the sacredness of their encounter. Emmy experiences a transformation of self that is a source of strength and serenity for years afterward, for she is able to integrate into her life the powerful forces that the experience awakens in her.

Faulkner's sense of the sacred is his awareness of the potential of human beings to experience the presence of a transcendent power of love and unity in the key experiences of self-discovery and growth that are a part of the natural process of life. The experience of the sacred is the result of the fusion of the spiritual and the physical, of the transcendent and the earthly, an experience that enables the person to be deeply appreciative of the preciousness of life.

It is in motherhood that Faulkner captures the quality of life that characterizes the whole person. His characterization of Lena Grove and of Dilsey is the key to his system of values, for both of them are able to integrate the life force into the texture of their lives and as a result to become resources for the nourishment and sustenance of life. For Faulkner the supreme value is human life, and whatever contributes to its growth and nourishment is to be treasured as sacred. Motherhood is symbolic of the human capacity for caring, for protecting, for treasuring, for loving life.

Faulkner portrays Lena and Dilsey, as well as Ruby Goodwin, Eula Snopes, and the woman in "Old Man," as sacred figures because they have integrated into their lives an ideal, creative, self-giving, life-sustaining love that springs from the very depths of their being. As a result, they possess a quality of transcendence and tranquility that flows from their eyes, their bodies, and their voices. Despite the lowliness of their places in life, they possess such a spirit of serenity and wholeness and such a capacity for love, creativity, and sustenance that other people are intensely aware of their power.

Lena Grove floats through life effortlessly; she accepts both her own mistakes and the hardships she faces with a sense of humor, and it seems that the natural process of life itself inevitably supplies her needs. Lena's tranquil journey is a source of delight because it is impulsive, spontaneous, free, trusting, and hopeful. Her attitude toward life is the result of her self-acceptance and her complete reliance on the resources of the power of life within her. She is committed to the search for her lover not out of her own need but for her child's sake. She obviously does not need so much to receive love as to give it, and she is deeply committed to loving and caring for the life that stirs in her womb. Nature itself supplies her with a man who is capable of the commitment she deserves because the life force that flows through her is so powerful and attractive that Byron Bunch cannot resist giving himself up to the journey of life to which her mere presence invites him. Faulkner's portrayal of Lena Grove captures all those qualities that Maslow identifies as characteristics of the self-actualized person—simplicity, effortlessness, joy, humor, aliveness, order, wholeness, beauty, playfulness, truth, honesty, and autonomy.[17]

In Dilsey, Faulkner embodies the strength of character and the endurance that are possible for human beings to achieve when their lives are dedicated to caring for others. Dilsey is a force of wholeness and order in the Compson household because she is able to love. Her love is not a needing or a selfish love, but a love for the Being of others, an unneeding and an unselfish love—the kind of love that Maslow describes as Being-cognition love.[18] What is the source of Dilsey's capacity for love? What gives her enough joy and resiliency of spirit to enable her to endure not out of effort and duty but out of a deep inner serenity and satisfaction? On the Easter Sunday morning that concludes *The Sound and the Fury*, Dilsey is burdened by age, the task of caring for others who never appreciate what she does, and the pain of having witnessed many deaths. As she is caught up in the preaching of the Negro minister, she experiences a mystical interlude in which she sees "the annealment of the blood of the remembered lamb." It is a vision that makes her say, "I've seed de first en de last. . . . I seed de beginnin, en now I sees de endin" (*S&F*, pp. 370–71). Dilsey's vision assures her of the truth of the Resurrection. The cycle of birth, death, and rebirth becomes powerfully real to her, and she experiences a sense of intimate contact with the world, the life process, and the structure of existence. In a flash, in a vision, she sees her life and the lives she has cared for as a whole, and she experiences the sense of coherence, completion, and fulfillment that enables her, despite all the pain and hardships of her existence, to believe that life is intrinsically worthwhile.[19] Dilsey's attitude toward human existence is like that which Maslow describes as characteristic of the self-actualized person—a "complete, loving, uncondemning, compassionate and perhaps amused acceptance of the world."[20] What could be a more accurate description of Faulkner's vision of life as it is embodied in the totality of his fiction?

It pleases me immensely that the last novel of Faulkner's career is *The Reivers*, for its vision of life is one of wisdom, acceptance, knowledge, and delight. Lucius Priest's initiation into life is productive and creative, for it ends with growth and regeneration. Lucius experiences pain and suffering and the trauma of his first encounter with sex, with violence, and with crime, but his initiation into human identity and his discovery of the essential truths of life take place under the guidance of reliable protectors. Though his friends lure him into the wild and frightening world of real life, Memphis, their own adventurous, loving, free spirits enable Lucius to encounter the realities of life with enthusiasm, courage, and hope. And, in the end, they are all able to be responsible. The words which Lucius's grandfather leave with him capture better than anything else in his fiction Faulkner's all-encompassing love of life:

> There are things, circumstances, conditions in the world which should not be there but are, and you cant escape them and indeed, you would not escape them even if you had the choice, since they too are a part of Motion, of participating in life, being alive. (*R.*, p. 155)

*The Reivers* concludes, of course, with the birth of a new Lucius Priest—Lucius Priest Hogganbeck—the assurance that the cycle of birth, growth, death, and rebirth will continue.

Lucius Priest's initiation experience enables him to integrate into his life those same values that Ike McCaslin learns in "The Bear," Faulkner's most famous story of initiation. Through personal encounter with the essential realities of life, Ike learns a code to live by that enables him to move through the process of initiation successfully and to achieve the quality of human being that is potentially alive in him.

Ike's deliberate and disciplined mastery of the woods—"every bayou, ridge, brake, landmark, tree and path"—represents his dedicated struggle for self-discovery and self-knowledge. The forest, as it is in Hawthorne's fiction, is symbolic of the unconscious self. Ike must wander through the maze; he must search the labyrinths of his own deepest self in order to discover who he is and to learn the essential truths of life. The bear symbolizes the wildness and power of the dynamic forces of the depths of the unconscious that are primitive, untamed, and potentially destructive, but also beautiful, immortal, and sacred. Ike must encounter that force directly without fear if he is to be whole. Sam Fathers is the loving and supportive mentor who teaches Ike to reverence the power the bear represents and who provides Ike with a set of values that will enable him to encounter the bear with courage and to grow through his experience.

From Sam Fathers, Ike learns that he must know the wilderness. Ike spends years acquiring the skill and knowledge that will make him worthy of even seeing the bear. He must be willing to give up the protection of civilization—his gun and his compass. He must trust himself enough to be able to confront the realities of the wilderness alone, relying only on his own inner resources. He must not only be willing to wait for a period of years to achieve his goal, but he must be willing to let go of time, to give himself up to wandering and searching. It is significant that when Ike finally experiences his moment of self-realization—when he risks his own life to save the brave little fyce—he sees the bear at last as he had always seen him in his dreams. It is a moment of truth and transcendence, a still point, in which Ike realizes in his life experience his potential being. Through his direct encounter with the powers of life and death, Ike comes to know inwardly the essential values of human life: "Courage, and honor, and pride, and pity, and love of justice and of liberty. They all touch the heart, and what the heart holds to becomes truth, as far as we know the truth."

Encounter with nature, birth, initiation, transformation, sexuality, creativity, and death were sacred experiences for ancient man because of his openness to the presence of a transcendent power in those events. Faulkner's fiction, I believe, recaptures this sense of the sacred dimension of these key events of life. Again and again his fiction demonstrates that as human beings are able to give themselves up to the motion of life and to open themselves to the dynamic powers of the life force that emerge from the unconscious self, they are able to experience transcendence in nature, in birth, in sexuality, in caring for others, in art and creativity, in any experience of learning about the essential truths of life, and in death. Indeed, Faulkner's fiction suggests, the potential for the experience of transcendence in these common, universal events is so powerful that the failure to be aware of their sacred dimension and to experience through them integration, wholeness, and regeneration results in an extreme sense of despair and alienation. These experiences are crucial steps in the growth process; the individual's need of the love, commitment, and support of others and of openness and trust of the cycle of these events is of crucial importance if regeneration is to take place. To know and to experience the presence of a transcendent power in the natural growth process enables human beings to achieve wholeness of self, a sense of the unity of life, and hope for the possibilities of the future.[21] Faulkner's fiction recaptures the ancient truth that the potential for wholeness and transcendence is radically present in the natural process of life, in the essential nature of human being, and in the very structure of Creation.

## Notes

1. Maslow, *Toward a Psychology of Being*, p. 206.
2. Maslow, *Religions, Values and Peak Experiences*, pp. 8–9.
3. Maslow, *Toward a Psychology of Being*, p. 206. See also Michael Polonyi, *Personal Knowledge*, William Poteat and Thomas Langford, eds., *Intellect and Hope*, and Abraham Heschel, *Who Is Man?*
4. Ibid., p. 10.
5. Ibid., p. 9.
6. Ibid.
7. "If our hope is to describe the world fully, a place is necessary for preverbal, ineffable, metaphorical, primary process, concrete-experience, intuitive and esthetic types of cognition, for there are

certain aspects of reality which can be cognized in no other way."
Ibid., p. 208.

8. "The very fact that through self-knowledge, i.e., by exploring
our own souls, we come upon the instincts and their world of
imagery should throw some light on the powers slumbering in the
psyche, of which we are seldom aware so long as all goes well. They
are potentialities of the greatest dynamism, and it depends entirely
on the preparedness and attitude of the conscious mind whether the
irruption of these forces and the images and ideas associated with
them will tend towards construction or catastrophe." C. G. Jung, *The
Undiscovered Self*, p. 119.

9. Maslow, *Religions, Values and Peak Experiences*, p. 42.

10. Maria-Gabriele Wosien, *Sacred Dance: Encounter With The
Gods*, p. 12.

11. *Early Prose and Poetry*, p. 92.

12. "The mystic state . . . produces a release of energy from the
unconscious which permits the actualization of man's highest potentialities." Andrew Greeley, *Ecstasy: A Way of Knowing*, p. 40.

13. Maslow, *Toward a Psychology of Being*, p. 15.

14. The peak experience is defined by Maslow as "a fusion of ego,
id, super-ego and ego-ideal, of conscious, pre-conscious and unconscious, of primary and secondary processes, a synthesizing of pleasure
principle with reality principle, a healthy regression without fear in the
service of the greatest maturity, a true integration of the person
at all levels." Ibid., p. 96.

15. Ibid., p. 73. See also p. 83 for Maslow's list of B-values. Cf.
Greeley, pp. 41–42.

16. Ibid., pp. 10–11.

17. Ibid., p. 83.

18. "B-love is welcomed into consciousness, and is completely
enjoyed. Since it is non-possessive, and is admiring rather than needing, it makes no trouble and is practically always pleasure-giving. . . .
In B-love there is a minimum of anxiety-hostility. For all practical
human purposes, it may even be considered to be absent. There *can*,
of course, be anxiety-for-the-other. In D-love one must always expect
some degree of anxiety-hostility. . . . Finally, I may say that B-love, in
a profound but testable sense, creates the partner. It gives him a
self-image, it gives him self-acceptance, a feeling of love-worthiness,
all of which permit him to grow. It is a real question whether the
full development of the human being is possible without it." Ibid., pp.
42–43.

19. Ibid., p. 88.
20. Ibid., p. 92.
21. "Research on . . . the universal mythology of the dream symbolism of death and rebirth indicates that a conviction of hopefulness is built into the structure of the human condition." Greeley, p. 62.

## six

Floyd C. Watkins

# Habet: Faulkner and the Ownership of Property

Isaac McCaslin's lyrical celebrations of the beauties of the wilderness and the frontier, his humanitarian idealism in his attitude toward slavery and the blacks, the apparent selflessness of his renunciation of his inheritance, and his willingness to give up sexual love and therefore children in his marriage have led many to regard him as a seer and a prophet. Indeed, one of his admirers asserts that he "has moved dangerously close to the person of the savior-god, to the person of Jesus: dangerously close, at least, for the purposes of fiction."[1] When Ike takes up carpentry, he associates the occupation with Christ and perhaps thinks of himself as Christ-like. He also regards the new world in religious terms as a second Eden. When God created the world and then again when he gave man America, a new world, "He created man to be His overseer on the earth and to hold suzerainty over the earth and the animals on it in His name, not to hold for himself and his descendants inviolable title forever, generation after generation, to the oblongs and squares of the earth, but to hold the earth mutual and intact in the communal anonymity of brotherhood . . ." (GDM, p. 257).[2] "Mutual"—the land is held by all equally; "intact"—it remains in one piece; "communal anonymity"—it is held without deeds or titles. Ike, then, does not believe in the ownership of the land or of large properties.

Some readers have taken this vision of a world without possession as Faulkner's own. Ike to one critic is "a symbol of the concept of natural rights as Faulkner seems to see it."[3] The South is cursed not only because of slavery but also because of its wrong relationship with property. It is said to be "cursed by the origins of its land titles and by the fact that the land is owned at all."[4] If this is Faulkner's view in his fiction, how is it reflected in his biography? He bought the ante-bellum Shegog house, took pride in repairing it, and renamed it Rowan Oak. Over a period of years he added several lots and built up one of the largest real estate holdings in or near Oxford. To protect his privacy on his property he put up a sign requesting that no one trespass without invitation. Certainly communal ownership did not prevail in his estates. When he lived in Virginia he bought a second home there and thus came to own two residences for one family. Furthermore, he bought a farm of 320 acres in northeastern Lafayette County, ran a commissary like that on the McCaslin and Edmonds plantation, and even kept records of money owed to him by Negro families—ledgers like those Ike read in the McCaslin commissary. Ike thought ownership was wrong. Faulkner was a lover of possessions—clothes, tools, or land. He owned properties like those Ike relinquished. How could a man of artistic integrity like Faulkner live in denial of the principles of his works? How could a possessor of properties believe that man is so perfect that he should live in communal ownership without deeds or titles? The answer, in my opinion, is that Faulkner did not agree with many of the ideas of Ike McCaslin.

Certainly William Faulkner never regarded himself as a social and political thinker creating in fiction patterns for the individual and society to follow. Nevertheless, in his writings man's relationship with his fellow man and with God is shown over and over again in terms of his concept of the ownership of property. Man must try to devise a system for dealing with the land whether it be communal, feudal, capitalistic, or communistic. The attitude toward ownership in Faulkner varies from character to character and to some extent from work to work. Indeed, it is never safe to conclude that Faulkner entirely agrees with a character or that a character's opinions are consistent throughout a work or in all the different stories about him. There are, however, three main attitudes toward property in Yoknapatawpha County: Ike's belief in communal ownership, which is almost invariably impractical for our world; selfish aggrandizement and exploitation—the evils of some of the Compsons, Thomas Sutpen, Flem Snopes; and the practice of holding and defending a reasonable quantity of property for the use of a man and his family and retainers. Faulkner's own conception of ownership is not always entirely consistent. In some works he seems to lapse momentarily into a nostalgic wish for a communal world that he knows can no longer exist. Almost invariably, however, he defends the individual's right to an "inviolable title" to land and property. The attitudes expressed in Faulkner's fiction agree with those of several Western philosophers before and during the establishment of the United States of America. Faulkner perhaps had not read Locke and Rousseau and others, but his ideas on the ownership of property were those of the best known thinkers among the founding fathers.

Communal ownership can exist only in a society that is primitive and usually also tribal. "God gave the World to Men in Common," according to John Locke, "but since he gave it them for their benefit, and the greatest Conveniences of Life they were capable to draw from it, it cannot be supposed he meant it should always remain in common and uncultivated."[5] For Locke as for Faulkner America was a figure for God's gift to man. "Thus in the beginning," Locke wrote, "all the World was America. . . ."[6] Communal ownership was important to the American Indian and in the origins of other racial and cultural groups in America as well: in Africa "land was held in common" by the Negro;[7] some American whites on the frontier held land either in communal ownership or without ownership at all; and the heritage of these three peoples is available to all. Thus the wilderness is "of the men, not white nor black nor red but men . . ." (*GDM*, p. 191). As Francis Weddel puts it in "Lo!" "God's forest and the deer which He put in it belongs to all" (*CS*, p. 401). Sam Fathers is the descendant of two tribal and communal peoples, African and Indian; and he passes on his tradition, or tries to, to Isaac McCaslin, a white. After the Civil War, Sam Fathers still lives according to the communal system in the wilderness; he "farmed no allotted acres of his own, as the other ex-slaves of old Carothers McCaslin did . . ." (*GDM*, p. 169). The concept of communal ownership was at one time a historical reality in America, and legal authorities write of how "Land was not conceived of in terms of individual private ownership and exclusive possession because Indian society stressed communal interests and sharing."[8]

Faulkner's lyrical creation of the qualities of an unspoiled wilderness has enticed readers to believe that man should strive to return to such a condition. The wilderness is sentient. After the hunters leave, their campsite heals in two weeks (*GDM*, p. 353). Even a dead tree heals "back into the earth" (*GDM*, p. 205). The land is a body; a sore heals; and a destroyed tree is a sore on a land that in Ike's youth is still healthy enough to get well. The wilderness not only affects the emotions of the hunters but also has emotions of its own. The big woods are "profound, sentient, gigantic and brooding" (*GDM*, p. 175). Several times Faulkner describes Ike's entry into the woods with a lyricism as delicate as that in Frost's "Stopping by Woods on a Snowy Evening." In "The Old People" the child Ike rides through a living landscape, "the wagon winding on among the tremendous gums and cypresses and oaks where no axe save that of the hunter ever sounded, between the impenetrable walls of cane and brier —the two changing yet constant walls just beyond which the wilderness whose mark he had brought away forever on his spirit even from that first two weeks seemed to lean, stooping a little, watching them and listening, not quite inimical because they were too small . . ." (*GDM*, pp. 176–77). The wilderness is an enormous presence: "it seemed to lean inward above them"; it stops breathing; and then when the hunters "become still, the wilderness breathed again" (*GDM*, p. 181). Ike may fail in establishing right ownership of land, but even when he enters the wilderness as an old man in "Delta Autumn" he still retains his sense of its beauty.

Despite the "communal anonymity of brotherhood" in a tribal society, the Indian did not live in a world of total benevolence.

No Edenic world ever really existed. Ikkemotubbe conspires among the Indians and murders before he sells the land, and God saw, Isaac says, "that only by voiding the land for a time of Ikkemotubbe's blood and substituting for it another blood, could He accomplish His purpose" (GDM, p. 259). It is not possible for the Indian to be true to his heritage and at the same time to sell the land. "When Ikkemotubbe discovered, realized, that he could sell it for money, on that instant it ceased ever to have been his forever, father to father to father, and the man who bought it bought nothing" (GDM, p. 257). In Ike's opinion he bought nothing because there was no title to convey and no way for one owner to act for all.

The land cannot be bought and sold according to the Indian's tribal rules, but the white man changes the system and establishes deeds and titles so that he can transfer land legally from owner to owner according to his new ways. Now man has been "dispossessed of Eden" (GDM, p. 257), as McCaslin Edmonds reminds Ike. Now man must assume his obligations and practice a different kind of morality. Thus Old Lucius Quintus Carothers McCaslin did own his property, and God as well as the white man allowed him to do so: "Grandfather did own the land nevertheless and notwithstanding because He permitted it, not impotent and not condoning and not blind because He ordered and watched it" (GDM, p. 258). The land as a whole does come into the possession not only of individual men but also of the white men as a people. America, Faulkner says in Requiem for a Nun, is "a white man's land; that was its fate, or not even fate but destiny, its high density in the roster of the earth" (RN, p. 42).

The precise moment of the conveyance of the native Indians' land to the usurping white man was for Faulkner one of the most meaningful, dramatic, and symbolic occasions in American history, a tragic moment but a necessary one. In the manner of a historian in Requiem for a Nun and in narrative accounts in a half dozen or so other works, Faulkner tells how the land was acquired from the Indians by the progenitors of the traditional families of his county—Carothers McCaslin, Louis Grenier,

Thomas Sutpen, and Jason Lycurgus Compson. The two men who bought a ford from the Indians in "Lo!" left no survivors. They buy the ford because, the Indian says, their people "find one side of a stream of water superior enough to the other to pay coins for the privilege of reaching it" (*CS*, p. 401). Each time an Indian tries to reestablish communal ownership by killing the purchaser. When the tribe goes to Washington for forgiveness from the Great White Father, they carry their Indian ways, and the confrontation between Indian primitiveness and Washington bureaucracy results in some of Faulkner's wildest farce.[9]

At the opposite extreme is the tragedy in *Absalom, Absalom!* Sutpen, Faulkner writes in *Requiem for a Nun*, "bought or proved on or anyway acquired a tract of land . . . and was apparently bent on establishing a place on an even more ambitious and grandiose scale than Grenier's . . ." (*RN*, pp. 39–40).

How he acquired it, the method of transferral from Indian to white, is left deliberately vague as a part of the mystery and rapacity of Sutpen. His treatment of the land is not vague. "*He tore violently a plantation*" "from the hundred square miles of tranquil and astonished earth . . . *tore violently*" (*AA*, pp. 8–9). Jason Lycurgus Compson is more sporting and less rapacious than Sutpen, but he also exploits the Indians and the land when he swaps a race-horse "for a square mile of what was to be the most valuable land in the future town of Jefferson . . ." (*RNE*, p. 18). The Compsons do not own too much land as Sutpen does, but they have problems with how they acquire it, use and do not use it, and dispose of it. As each character is unique in the way he acquires and develops his land, so the families of Yoknapatawpha show what they are by their relationship to land and property. The history of the Compson place is the history of a family. Jason Lycurgus Compson sells the land for Jefferson to the city fathers at a dear price; Jason III sells more of it for one son to go to Harvard and to pay for his daughter's wedding. And finally Jason IV sells the land to Flem Snopes, who cuts it up into lots for a subdivision.

The white man at various times and places has also held the land communally as the Indians did. Strangely, perhaps, the most prominent white character who lived in such a primitive world becomes later one of the chief exploiters, Thomas Sutpen. The meanings of *Absalom, Absalom!* and *Go Down, Moses* are in some ways mirror images of each other. Sutpen in the mountains of western Virginia lives in communal ownership if not in brotherhood. There are no property lines and no titles there, where Sutpen "had never heard of, never imagined, a place, a land divided neatly up and actually owned by men . . ." (*AA*, p. 221). There "the land belonged to anybody and everybody . . ." (*AA*, p. 221). Sutpen lives in a society with the same concept of property that the Indian and McCaslin had. Fences and ownership do not exist among these people as they did not among the Indians in "Lo!" "The man who would go to the trouble and work to fence off a piece of it and say 'This is mine' was crazy . . ." (*AA*, p. 221). Sutpen's western Virginia is an imperfect and savage world of drunkenness and violence, but it is innocent of the right of property.

To migrate from that mountain world to the Tidewater plantations is to learn of ownership. Twice Faulkner describes the move as a fall: "He fell into it. . . . They fell into it, the whole family . . ." (*AA*, p. 222). It seems almost to be a fall without an Eden to fall from. Sutpen has come into a world of exploitative ownership of vast tracts of land and large numbers of slaves. He has been able to conceive of the individual's ownership of so small and basic a thing as a rifle (*AA*, pp. 228–29), but he is compelled to learn of a world where "You got to have land and niggers and a fine house . . ." (*AA*, p. 238). He attempts to adopt such a belief in ownership for himself, and figuratively at least he fences off a hundred square miles. His own selfish misuses of property and human beings derive in part from this sudden change from one world to another and from communal ownership to another system.

If Sutpen falls from a primitive world, Ike McCaslin would like to do just the opposite—to regain communal anonymity. He is a believer in the Rousseauistic and romantic concept of the nature of society and civilization. "The first person who, having enclosed a piece of ground," Rousseau wrote, "bethought of saying, *This is mine*, and found people simple enough to believe him, was the real founder of civil society." Fencing property caused "crimes, battles and murders—. . . horrors and misfortunes."[10] Ike connects slavery and the land as Rousseau and Locke did. That slavery is associated with the right of property and ought not to be is also consistent with John Locke's thinking: "Though the earth, and all inferior Creatures be common to all Men, Yet every man has a *Property* in his own *Person*. This nobody has any Right to but himself. The *Labour* of his Body and *Work* of his Hands, we may say, are properly his."[11] The point is not merely that Faulkner may have been following Rousseau and Locke; he and Ike McCaslin were thinking about an archetypal problem in man's conception and definition of himself. If Ike would like the world to remain in an ideal state of nature, the corrupters of the principles of the ownership of land in Faulkner also may be described in Rousseau's terms: "In fine, insatiable ambition, the thirst of raising their respective fortunes, not so much from real want as from the desire of surpassing others, must inspire all mankind with a vile propensity to injure each other. . . ."[12]

Ike is not the only character in Faulkner who fails because of his desire to escape the curses of slavery and property. As he fails tragically, his father and uncle, Uncle Buck and Uncle Buddy, fail comically. They move out of the big colonial house because their father had built it with slave labor. Since they wish to free themselves from the taint of slavery, they build their "one-room log cabin" (*GDM*, p. 262)— it has two rooms in a different story (*UNV*, p. 52)—and they refuse "to allow any slave to touch any timber of it" (*GDM*, p. 262). But the falseness of their hope and effort is shown by their inability to build the cabin without help from slavery. Slaves help them raise the logs that are too heavy for just two men. Their inability to escape the curse of slavery and the use of the big house or the ownership of property is also shown by Uncle Buck's moving back into the big house after his comic courtship and marriage to Sophonsiba Beauchamp (*GDM*, p. 301).

Faulkner's attitude toward communal ownership was not

always entirely negative and hostile. In *The Unvanquished* Uncle Buck and Uncle Buddy believe "that land did not belong to the people but that people belonged to land and that the earth would permit them to live on and out of it and use it only so long as they behaved . . ." (*UNV*, p. 54). And Colonel Sartoris, almost an arch capitalist, says approvingly that "they were ahead of their time . . ." (*UNV*, p. 54). They also have "ideas about social relationship that maybe fifty years after they were both dead people would have a name for" (*UNV*, p. 54). During the Civil War they persuade their neighbors "to pool their little patches of poor hill land along with the niggers and the McCaslin plantation," and as a result "their women and children did have shoes . . ." (*UNV*, p. 55). This seems to be a temporary system of communal ownership, and it achieves good economic effects as well as a cooperative neighborliness or brotherhood. It is more admirable than Ike's relinquishment. It preserves the actual right of property and the integrity of ownership. A similar condition prevails in the dividing and the sharing of the mules and property that Granny Millard gets back from the Yankee army—an instance of neighborliness and brotherhood also during the conditions of war.

Even though communal ownership is not possible in a civilized state, Faulkner himself still ardently yearned for a world without elaborate legal systems and complex social agreements and contracts. Simplicity is ideal even though it is impossible. Faulkner desired the simple and the oral agreement rather than the elaborate and the written. An agreement between two people, he believed, is more sacred than the complicated workings of institutions and governments. Once he said he would honor an agreement more than a contract (Blotner, p. 1180). As country people put it, a man's word is his bond. In financial dealings with agents who sold his fiction and with motion picture companies, Faulkner's oral contracts frequently resulted in misunderstandings. The more complicated the system, the less he seemed to believe the individual was obligated to honor a contract. Consequently he freely violated a contract with a Hollywood company, and on at least one occasion he dishonestly broke another.[13] His admiration of a simple society, a system just slightly removed from communal ownership, may be the cause of his attitude. In "Old Man" the cajun and the convict agree to share the proceeds of their alligator hunting in a contract more primitive even than language. "Two people who could not even talk to one another made an agreement which both not only understood but which each knew the other would hold true and protect (perhaps for this reason) better than any written and witnessed contract" (*WP*, p. 260). This informal agreement establishes a kind of innocent society that apparently William Faulkner as well as the convict and Ike McCaslin would admire.

Faulkner's yearning for simplicity and the independence of ownership make him almost as extreme as Isaac McCaslin in his distrust of government, business, institutions, and almost any organizations. Modern government destroys relationships with property; relief agencies like the WPA, for example, cause corruption by making men "lie about and conceal the ownership of land and property in order to hold relief jobs which they have no intention of performing . . ." (*CS*, p. 46). Regulatory government agencies also interfere with the right of property and establish a wrong relationship with property when they "try to tell a man how he cant raise his own cotton whether he will or wont" (*GDM*, p. 339; see also *CS*, 55).

Characters who own no property are usually shiftless and evil. Not to own property, according to Major de Spain is just quitting (*GDM*, p. 309). In *Go Down, Moses* the lynchers and the violent mobs are made up of "barbers and garage mechanics and deputy sheriffs and mill-and-gin-hands and powerplant firemen," and all of these are the landless of the earth (*GDM*, p. 290). Those who live in boarding houses or in an "empty rented room" (GDM, p. 315) like Ike McCaslin have no relationship with property. Boarders live together and have the accouterments of a family without meaningful family relationships. Those who live without property in a world of property-owners are exploited, and in turn they exploit the owners. Barn burning is the supreme lawless violation of the right of property in the farming society of *The Hamlet*, and Ab Snopes, who burns de Spain's barn, is a tenant rather an owner. As Cash Bundren says, "I don't reckon nothing excuses setting fire to a man's barn and endangering his stock and destroying his property. That's how I reckon a man is crazy" (*AILD*, p. 510).

The most sensational characters in Faulkner are the exploiters. They usually begin in a communal society as Sutpen does and in poverty. Because they have no contentment with a reasonable amount of possessions, they quickly amass land and wealth by extreme aggrandizement. Or they cease hunting communally and try to seize all the game for themselves. Boon Hogganbeck exists in the wilderness almost communally, cared for by the hunters and even by a boy when he must go to a city. The moment the world changes, he hunts alone and entirely for self. Boon under the tree full of squirrels at the end of "The Bear" is a representation of a way of life exactly opposite to his old life in the camp.

Exploiters are either frontiersmen like Jason Lycurgus Compson and Sutpen or unprincipled tradesmen like Jason Compson IV or Flem Snopes. They rape the land, their communities, and America. The frontiersmen in *Requiem for a Nun* are "without bowels for avarice or compassion or forethought either, changing the face of the earth: felling a tree which took two hundred years to grow, in order to extract from it a bear or a capful of wild honey . . ." (*RN*, p. 102). And he accomplishes his own extinction, "haunting the fringes of the wilderness which he himself had helped to destroy . . ." (*RN*, p. 103). As they treated the land, "vanquished the wilderness," they treated the people, "even stepped into the very footgear of them they dispossessed" (*RN*, p. 218). The husbandman destroys "the milieu in which alone the forest man could exist" (*RN*, p. 218). The evils of the modern are even greater than the destruction on the frontier.

The good people in Faulkner's fiction own property, and they have a right relationship with the land and property. They may not rightly own a quantity of land or property that is so great that the people who live on it exist in a relationship of exploiter and exploited. Sutpen's hundred square miles is by its very size, I believe, immoral. But large holders and small holders and even renters may have proper attitudes toward property.

Two large landholders who are admirable are Major de Spain and McCaslin Edmonds. The Major is generous with the wilderness he owns. His generosity is the opposite of exploitation. He shares with his fellow huntsmen, and he also welcomes the swampers to shoot game on his land and before his dogs.

McCaslin, or Cass, Edmonds is the chief advocate of Faulkner's own philosophy of the individual's right of property. His eminent rightness has not been sufficiently noticed, however, perhaps because he is not the protagonist of the work and because in some criticism he has been regarded as the advocate of a selfish theory in contrast to what is thought to be the selflessness of Ike. McCaslin believes that one must own the land, assume the obligation, and be responsible for the guilt. Lucius Quintus Carothers McCaslin established a relationship to the property that Ike was obligated to continue. Old McCaslin "saw the opportunity and took it, bought the land, took the land, got the land no matter how, held it to bequeath, no matter how, out of the old grant, the first patent, when it was a wilderness of wild beasts and wilder men, and cleared it, translated it into something to bequeath to his children, worthy of bequeathment for his descendants' ease and security and pride and to perpetuate his name and accomplishments" (*GDM*, p. 256). McCaslin Edmonds admits old Carothers McCaslin did wrong, but along with the wrong he also did right. Despite his evil, he was human. Ike, on the contrary, by refusing to own the land becomes nothing. Richard Adams has put the point well: "We must try to save ourselves and one another by being involved with one another in responsible actions that will acknowledge the errors and the guilt, and that will build something better in the present and for the future."[14]

Small ownership is as admirable as possession of vast estates, in some ways even more so. At least in part Faulkner would subscribe to John Locke's belief that "As much as any one can make use of to any advantage of life before it spoils; so much he may by his labour fix a Property in. Whatever is beyond this is more than his share, and belongs to others."[15] The small holder in Faulkner takes much personal pride in having earned his property by the sweat of his brow in Biblical terms. Cash objects strongly to Darl's burning the barn because he destroyed "what a man has built with his own sweat and stored the fruit of his sweat into" (*AILD*, p. 228). For Cash also, quality and craftsmanship are more important than quantity of holdings: "It's like some folks has the smooth, pretty boards to build a courthouse with and others don't have no more than rough lumber fitten to build a chicken coop. But it's better to build a tight chicken coop than a shoddy courthouse . . ." (*AILD*, p. 224). Yeomen farmers like the Quicks, the Tulls, the Armstids (except in *The Hamlet*), and the Bundrens have a good relationship with property. They own their own home, a team, a cow, and the necessities for a yeoman family in their time. Anse's laziness, however, makes him irresponsible somewhat in the manner of Ike McCaslin. Jewel's love of his horse is a proper attitude toward property even though the poverty of his world forced him to earn the horse with inordinate work. His giving up his horse for the family is a generosity. The yeoman MacCallum family in the short stories and *Sartoris* are among the most attractive people in Faulkner, and they are an embodiment of Faulkner's belief that one should fiercely protect his independence from bureaucratic threats to property rights. The number of characters who have a really good relationship to property is not great, but they are sufficient to establish Faulkner's conception of what that relationship should be in a world where it is difficult for man to be what he should be.

Owning the land is not the only proper relationship one may have with it. Negroes especially live on the land with love even though they rent rather than possess. "Love of the land without the desire to possess, alter, or despoil it preserves the integrity of Faulkner's Negroes. . . ."[16] Both Rider and Lucas Beauchamp establish a home and build a fire on the hearth of a house on property owned by the Edmondses. Lucas possessed "the use and benefit of the land with none of the responsibilities" (*GDM*, p. 44), and the house belongs to him though he has no deed. Possession of this kind comes from a man's having been born on the land and having worked on it and hunted on it. Lucas's relationship to possessions other than land is also what it should be. Like Cash, he takes "a solid pride in having good tools to use" (*GDM*, p. 42).

But Lucas does not always have a proper attitude toward property. He falls when he attempts to find one thousand dollars with his gold-finding machine. His wife and Roth Edmonds know "what it might do to him . . ." (*GDM*, p. 122). Property is labor, and finding gold would not be establishing a proper title. It is "the curse of God" because there was "no sweat, at least none of his own" (*GDM*, p. 123). Lucas's search is like that of three others who seek unearned property—Ratliff, Bookwright, and Armstid at the end of *The Hamlet*. But Lucas gives up his machine and is not defeated as Armstid was. The theme of the relationship to property in "The Fire and the Hearth" helps to unify *Go Down, Moses* by providing a commentary by example on Ike's relinquishment.

One does not go to Faulkner to find the course of history and particularly American history in his works. Faulkner has not contributed significantly to the thinking about the state of nature and the origins of government in Hobbes, Locke, and Rousseau. Nor has he advanced new cultural and historical interpretations of the state of nature and the frontier in America. Rather, his province is fiction, and he has created it in terms of the peculiarly American experience. His characters are uniquely individual. The bad ones usurp the property, the labor, and the rights of others; and then they standardize the world. The weak ones relinquish their rights and responsibilities. In historical, epical, and religious terms, the good people in Faulkner establish their individuality with their possessions. Good people cannot return to a communal system or survive spiritually under a standardized system of aggrandizement. The only survival in Faulkner's world with integrity lies in the possession of a somewhat limited quantity of uniquely individual possessions.

## NOTES

1. R. W. B. Lewis, *The Picaresque Saint* (Philadelphia: J. B. Lippincott Co., First Keystone Edition, 1961), p. 209.

2. The following texts of Faulkner's works and the abbreviations for them are used in this article:

*As I Lay Dying* (New York: The Modern Library, 1967). *AILD*.

*Absalom, Absalom!* (New York: Random House, 1936). *AA*.

*Collected Stories* (New York: Random House, 1943). *CS*.

*Go Down, Moses and Other Stories* (New York: Random House, 1942). *GDM*.

*Requiem for a Nun* (New York: Random House, 1951). *RN*. (London: Chatto and Windos, 1957). *RNE*.

*The Unvanquished* (New York: Random House, 1938). *UNV*.

*The Wild Palms* (New York: Random House, 1939). *WP*.

3. Dale G. Breadin, "William Faulkner and the Land," *American Quarterly*, 10 (Fall 1958), 349.

4. Breadin, p. 347.

5. John Locke, *Two Treatises of Government*, ed. Peter Laslett (Cambridge, At the University Press), p. 309.

6. Ibid., p. 319.

7. John W. Blassingame, *The Sense of Community: Plantation Life in the Antebellum South* (New York: Oxford University Press, 1972), p. 12.

8. James R. Kerr, "Constitutional Rights, Tribal Justice, and the American Indian," *Journal of Public Law*, 18 (1969), 314.

9. M. E. Bradford, "Faulkner and the Great White Father," *Louisiana Studies*, 3 (Winter 1964), 324 ff.

10. J. J. Rousseau, *The Miscellaneous Works* (London, 1767), I, 213.

11. Locke, pp. 305–06.

12. Rousseau, p. 230.

13. Joseph Blotner, *Faulkner: A Biography* (New York: Random House, 1974), pp. 1193, 1124.

14. Richard P. Adams, "Focus on William Faulkner's 'The Bear,': Moses and the Wilderness," in David Madden, *American Dreams, American Nightmares* (Carbondale: Southern Illinois Univ. Press), p. 135.

15. Locke, p. 308.

16. John M. Ditsky, "Uprooted Trees: Dynasty and the Land in Faulkner's Novels," *Tennessee Studies in Literature*, 17 (1972), 153.

# William Faulkner and William Butler Yeats: Parallels and Affinities

In Faulkner's "The Old People," Isaac McCaslin undergoes his initiation into the code of the wilderness. He ceases "to be a child and [becomes] a hunter and a man."[1] After he has killed his first buck and has been anointed  on the forehead with its "hot smoking blood"[2] by Sam Fathers, the officiating priest of the rite, something else happens to Isaac: later on that afternoon he has a vision of a great antlered buck that must have been, as later events indicate, a ghost, not a flesh-and-blood animal.

Isaac is troubled by the phenomenon and refuses to believe that the buck was merely a figment of his imagination. That night he describes his experience to his elder cousin, McCaslin Edmonds, and though McCaslin listens to him quietly Isaac suddenly bursts out: "You don't believe it. I know you don't—." But McCaslin reassures the boy. Why shouldn't the slain animals who have never had "enough time about the earth" haunt the "places still unchanged from what they were when the blood used and pleasured in them . . . ?"[3] And when the boy, still not quite satisfied, cries out: "But I saw it," his kinsman says: "I know you did! So did I. Sam took me in there once after I killed my first deer."[4]

William Butler Yeats too has something to report about a phantom deer. In his "General Introduction for My Work," Yeats tells of a gamekeeper on Lady Augusta Gregory's estate

139

at Coole who "heard the footsteps of a deer on the edge of the lake where no deer had passed for a hundred years. . . ."[5]

A trivial and inconsequential coincidence? Perhaps so, but note what Yeats goes on to say by way of accounting for the century-dead buck's walking by the lake. A certain cracked old priest, he tells us, gave out that

> nobody had been to hell or heaven in his time. . . . that the dead stayed where they had lived, or near it, sought no abstract region of blessing or punishment but retreated, as it were, into the hidden character of the neighbourhood.[6]

Now the explanation offered by the cracked old priest is not remarkably different from McCaslin Edmonds' way of accounting for the phantom deer's haunting the earth. Recall what McCaslin told the young Ike:

> . . . you can't be alive forever, and you always wear out life long before you have exhausted the possibilities of living. And all that must be somewhere; all that could not have been invented and created just to be thrown away. . . . Besides, what would it want . . . knocking around out there [under the icy stars], when it never had enough time about the earth as it was, when there is plenty of room about the earth, plenty of places still unchanged from what they were when the blood used and pleasured in them while it was still blood?[7]

True, McCaslin is talking about the animals not wanting to leave the earth that they had loved, whereas the old cracked priest—even though Yeats refers to him in the immediate context of his remarks about the ghostly deer—is surely talking principally about human beings.

But in the world imagined by Faulkner, McCaslin's reasoning about the animals' yearning to stay close to the earth on which they had lived also applies to human beings. Think of Faulkner's beautiful and moving story "Pantaloon in Black." The wife of a young black man named Rider has suffered an untimely death. After her body has been put in the grave, the bereaved husband starts to walk back to the cabin in which they had spent their few months of happiness. But his friends and kinsfolk try to dissuade him. One of them says, awkwardly enough,

> what he had not intended to say, what he had never conceived of himself saying in circumstances like these, even though everyone knew it—the dead . . . either will not or cannot quit the earth yet although the flesh they once lived in has been returned to it, let the preachers tell and reiterate and affirm how [the dead] left [the earth] not only without regret but with joy, mounting toward glory. . . .[8]

and so Rider's friend, almost in spite of himself, does blurt it out: "You dont wants ter go back dar. She be wawkin yit."

Mannie, Rider's dead wife, *is* walking. Rider sees her for a moment quite plainly when he enters their cabin, but she quickly fades, as heartbreakingly as Eurydice faded before the anguished eyes of Orpheus.

A courteous devil's advocate among you may have some questions to put. I can imagine him asking: Well, if one grants the parallels that you've cited between Yeats and Faulkner, one must still ask: what is the point? We all know that Yeats was notoriously given to esoteric studies, was a member of the Order of the Golden Dawn, and belonged to Madame Blavatsky's inner circle of devotees. That Yeats should have seriously reported spiritualistic nonsense is hardly surprising. But isn't Faulkner's case quite different? Oxford, Mississippi, at most could scarcely have yielded anything more sinister than a half-dozen ouija boards, or have boasted the presence of even one lonely member of the Rosicrucian Order who, if he existed, probably was no more than a mail-order member, having answered in hopefulness or hopelessness the modest advertisement he had seen on a back page of a copy of *Argosy* magazine or *Western Stories* picked up at Chisholm's drugstore on the square. Is there any genuine relation between Yeats's concern for ghostly happenings and the fact that Faulkner endowed some of his characters with a nature mystique?

Such a set of questions would be fairly put, and I shall try to be equally honest in my answers. My point in calling attention to parallels between Yeats and Faulkner has little to do with whether Yeats seriously believed in spiritual phenomena. W. H. Auden once told me that although T. S. Eliot had had real visions about which he very rarely talked, Yeats talked about his all the time, though Auden doubted that Yeats had ever experienced one in his entire life. Be that as it may, such is not the matter of my concern here. Nor am I concerned with whether Faulkner really believed in revenants and hauntings. What interests me in both men is their warm and sympathetic appreciation of men who did literally believe in supernatural happenings. Though Yeats extended his interests far afield—to the writers of Hermes Trismegistus, the medieval alchemists, and the Cabalists, his direct hold on the esoteric traditions was through the legendary past of Ireland, and through his first-hand acquaintance with the Irish peasantry. Faulkner had a comparable resource in the genuine folk culture that existed in the rural South. A fruitful comparison of Yeats and Faulkner must proceed from a recognition of the general parallels between the provincial cultures that nourished the genius of both men.

I would stress the importance of their provincial cultures by insisting on the differences between their personalities. Otherwise, a hasty glance might in fact prompt the question: what do these two distinguished writers have in common except their Nobel Prizes? Yeats, with his flowing tie and carefully disarranged hair, Yeats, the friend of such decadent poets as Edward Dowson and Lionel Johnson, Yeats of *The Yellow Book* and the Cheshire Cheese—what possible affinities could there be between this late romantic, son of a distinguished pre-Raphaelite painter, and William Faulkner, who was long content to be the ne'er-do-well Count No-Count, Faulkner who was sometimes seen wearing "mismatched shoes" and with "the elbows out of his coat," Faulkner, the dreamy young man, the jest of his friends and sometimes the despair of his family, who lacked a respectable job. I cheerfully admit the real and great differences between the two men. Indeed, I shall go further: I shall dimiss as of no special consequence for my argument that Yeats very early became Faulkner's favorite poet. My basic thesis has little to do with Faulkner's reading of Yeats or any attempt on his part to imitate his poetry. What I shall stress will be the parallels between the cultures out of which Yeats and Faulkner came.

To return to the folk cultures of Ireland and the South: A vigorous folk culture itself implies a number of other parallel features—conservatism, old-fashioned customs and ideas, a paternalistic system centered in an aristocracy or at least a land-owning squirearchy. In short, a folk society based on the land implies the Big House with landed proprietors and the ethos that goes with such a governing class as part of the larger cultural continuum in which the folk subsists.

The particular details of the cultural situation as between Ireland and the Old South were, as we would expect, vastly different. In the American South there were both whites and blacks, and though at points they shared a common culture, they were separated by a caste barrier. One effect of the caste barrier was to mitigate somewhat the rigors of a class system. In one sense, all the whites stood together despite the class barriers that existed within the white society. That fact, and the persistence of the frontier virtues in the Old Southwest, operated to unite the whites. At all events, in Faulkner's novels people of yeoman stock such as V. K. Ratliff have a truly friendly relation with the likes of Harvard-educated Gavin Stevens; young Bayard Sartoris is on easy terms with the admirable MacCallum family, and even the "gaunt, malaria-ridden" swampers, when they meet up with Major de Spain on the annual bear hunt, are greeted in friendly fashion. Their spokesman speaks with some diffidence, explaining that "We figgered we'd come up and watch, if you don't mind." The Major replies at once: "You are welcome. You are welcome to shoot. He's more your bear than ours."[9]

The black folk constituted, to be sure, a special case, but out in the country, at least, the old patriarchal system had enough slack in it to allow the development of human relations between plantation owner and black tenant: witness Lucas Beauchamp and Roth Edmonds, or Bayard Sartoris and the black family with whom he finds shelter on Christmas Eve. Much more to the point, of course, is Faulkner's own attitude as man and as artist.

He writes without condescension or disparagement about the yeoman whites, about the landless whites, and about the almost always landless blacks. I don't mean to say that he sentimentalizes men because they were deprived. He knows a Snopes when he sees one. But he rarely falls into cuteness or folksiness, or the other vices of local colorism.

The gap between both Yeats and Faulkner and their respective folk cultures clearly existed—and however important it is that the writers' human sympathies did bridge the gap, the fact of the gap is important. Though Yeats as a writer needed the world of the Irish folk, he also needed a certain detachment from it—a certain distance—in order to be able to articulate what he saw and felt. He needed to have a knowledge of history, literature, and philosophy—to be able to stand at a window opening on the great outside world. To be totally immersed in the world of the folk is to become only partially articulate—to become an instance of the folk culture rather than a voice for its aspirations or an interpreter of its meaning. However important Ireland was for Yeats, the artist, the great outside world was essential for him too.

I speak of Yeats, but all that I have said applies fully to Faulkner. What was crucial for both men was the fact that, in spite of their necessary detachment from County Sligo, Ireland, or Lafayette County, Mississippi, neither was insulated from his local culture; thus, it could become for him an enormously valuable resource.

In developing one aspect of the cultural situation common to Yeats and Faulkner, I have already implied a number of others. Perhaps a sensible strategy at this point would be to make some of them explicit, thus developing and clarifying the cultural context out of which they came and upon which they drew. In the first place, that context contained the large landholder as distinguished from the small holder and, of course, the landless. As for the middle class, in the west of Ireland it was small; in late nineteenth century north Mississippi, it was considerably larger. In this connection, one must be cautious in using the term "aristocracy," for it can be misleading, particularly as applied to Faulkner's country. In Ireland, of course, many of the large landholders were titled, like Yeats's friend Lady Augusta Gregory. But even, with Ireland, I believe it would be safer to refer, not to the aristocratic tradition, but to the tradition of the Big House. In north Mississippi, the big house was, of course, the plantation house, not nearly so large, however, as the manor houses of Ireland or even some of those to the south in the Natchez country or the great sugarcane plantations in Louisiana. In any case, the members of plantation stock in north Mississippi were relative newcomers to the land, a sort of country gentry or squirearchy, who may have achieved substantial property in one or two generations, in much shorter time than the country families of the Virginia Tidewater or the Low Country around Charleston, and of course much more recently than those families that occupied the Big Houses of Ireland.

Yeats, by the way, though proud of his connection with the Butler family, and sharp in his condemnation of the tradesmen and the hucksters, admitted that "the family of Yeats" were "never more than small gentry."[10] His father was a painter; his father's father a country parson. Nor were Faulkner's more immediate forebears great plantation owners. His great-grandfather, the Old Colonel, walked into the state from Tennessee as a penniless boy. In the almost frontier world of north Mississippi of the 1830s and 1840s, he rapidly became a pillar of the community, in due time built and owned a short-line railroad, made the grand tour of Europe, and had some success as a novelist. He had become a leader in the community; his great-grandson was proud of the fact that the Old Colonel was "part of Stonewall Jackson's left at 1st Manassas."[11]

Donald Torchiana remarks that what attracted Yeats to the tradition of the Anglo-Irish landholders of eighteenth-century Protestant Ireland "was more [a] quality of intellect than any necessary class distinction." Certainly what Yeats valued in Lady Gregory was not her title nor her wealth—which, in fact, was not great. It was rather her courage, self-discipline, magnanimity, courtesy, graciousness—in short, the aristocratic virtues. This was what he had in mind in his celebrated speech to the Irish Senate, when he said of his own forebears, the Anglo-Irish:

we "are no petty people. We are one of the greatest stocks of Europe."[12] The individuals whom he cited—Burke, Grattan, Swift, Parnell—were not men of wealth but of selfless devotion to the state; and what Yeats went on to praise as the special contributions of his people to Ireland were "literature" and "political intelligence."

Such too, were the qualities and virtues that Faulkner admired in the Old South. There are no plaster saints in Faulkner's pantheon, nor are there fake aristocrats. The virtues displayed by "Old Bayard" Sartoris, by his Aunt Jenny Du Pre, by Mrs. Rosa Millard, and by Uncle Buck and Uncle Buddy, are essentially the virtues of V. K. Ratliff and of Lucas Beauchamp, for in Faulkner's world the yeoman white and the black man can, in their own terms, qualify as "aristocrats."

Faulkner's "aristocrats" have, it is true, the defects of their virtues. Col. Sartoris is irascible, given to violence, proud, ambitious, and vindictive—though he is never mean or petty and he is absolutely fearless. (One could use very nearly these same words to describe the black man Lucas Beauchamp). Drusilla Hawk's aristocratic virtues become perverted: she is dauntless, but in her worship of honor and courage, she has forgotten pity, compassion, and even her womanhood. She is willing to send her step-son to his probable death, not because of grief for her slain husband, but because she is utterly fascinated by the notion of death (or risk of death) in defense of some abstract conception of masculine honor.

Horace Benbow, too, exhibits the aristocratic virtues only partially and in defect. That is to say, Horace is a man of honor; he is magnanimous, public-spirited, eager to promote justice. He sincerely wants to secure the acquital of Lee Goodwin; he is genuinely shocked when Lee's wife offers her body to him in payment of the fee that she is confident any lawyer would ask. But Horace is naive; he underestimates the power of evil. When it comes to women, he is weak and pliable—with his wife Belle and with his sister Narcissa. He cannot be brought to realize that few people in the modern world possess either honor or decency and that many lack respect for such virtues in others.

Narcissa is no aristocrat at all, having lost the virtues that should have come to her from her forebears. She is a selfish, calculating woman, completely in thrall to bourgeois respectability —and Faulkner almost rivals Yeats in his detestation of the bourgeois concern to keep up appearances. Narcissa doesn't care whether Lee Goodwin hangs or not. She simply objects to her brother's having taken the case of a common bootlegger accused of murder. So she sells out her brother to the district attorney and thus insures Lee Goodwin's death, just as later[13] she offers her body to the Federal agent in return for letters that he holds —anonymous, obscene letters written to her years before. Nobody will ever know that she slept with the agent; thus she chooses fornication in fact rather than risk the possibility that strangers might read letters to her proposing a fornication that never took place. Such is respectability. As an "aristocrat," Narcissa Benbow Sartoris is a whited sepulchre. But it is I who borrow the Biblical phrase. What Faulkner actually wrote of her was this: she "looked full at [Horace] . . . with that serene and stupid impregnability of heroic statuary; she was in white."[14]

The district attorney to whom Narcissa sells out Horace has no claim to the aristocratic virtues by background or nurture, and even if he had, he would have long ago repudiated them. Faulkner describes him as a "young man with a word for everyone and a certain alert rapacity about the eyes."[15] In his college days, he had gained a reputation for cheating at poker, but when he talks with Narcissa about the sell-out, he is a straight law-and-order man. We must not, however, linger over Eustace Graham. He is a common enough shyster lawyer with political ambitions. A more nearly final case is Faulkner's Flem Snopes. He is utterly without honor, completely avaricious, and scarcely human in his absolute devotion to making money. Faulkner apparently regards it as natural and appropriate that Flem should show a great concern for respectability. (Today we would say that Flem is acutely aware of his "public image.") Flem is the mercantile spirit walking around on two legs as he remorselessly chews his worthless quid of gum.

Yeats, too, carried on a life-long quarrel with the bourgeoisie.

The objects of his affection were the country gentlemen and the peasant, the artist, and the saint. His valedictory poem urges the Irish poets of the future to

> Sing the peasantry, and then
> Hard-riding country gentlemen.
> The holiness of monks, and after
> Porter-drinkers' randy laughter. . . .[16]

In one of his poems he urges Lady Gregory to accept the inevitability of defeat in any competition with men who are honorless:

> Be secret and take defeat
> From any brazen throat,
> For how can you compete,
> Being honour bred, with one
> Who, were it proved he lies,
> Were neither shamed in his own
> Nor in his neighbours' eyes?[17]

Yeat's harshest lines are reserved for those mean and narrow-minded people who

> . . . fumble in a greasy till
> And add the half-pence to the pence

until they have

> . . . dried the marrow from the bone.

In was in consideration of the number of such petty hucksters that Yeats uttered his famous lines,

> Romantic Ireland's dead and gone,
> It's with O'Leary in the grave.[18]

Later on, Yeats was moved, principally by the events of the Easter Rebellion of 1916, to revise his despairing verdict, though he never ceased to resent the bourgeois ethic, which he believed was inimical to all that was high-hearted, passionate, and heroic. A close look at his career reveals a continuing alteration of love and loathing for his native land, a conflict that closely parallels Faulkner's love-hate relation with his native region.

Faulkner never said so in so many words—not, at least, any that I have found—that the romantic South was dead and gone. But some of the older characters in his fiction occasionally express this view, and in general the ethos of Faulkner's stories and novels reflects that of an older, more heroic society. Moreover, the clear import of Faulkner's observation that the prime question now was whether the Snopeses were going to take over the country is that the older aristocratic code was under attack and might not survive.

Yet the strength of Faulkner's work is that even less than Yeats did he risk sentimentalizing the life of the gentry or of declaiming their virtues in his own voice. Rather, the code is implicit, both positively and negatively, in the speeches and actions of Faulkner's characters.

At this point it may be useful to pause for a kind of summation of what has been said and to spell out some of the further implications. The kind of culture that I have thus far described is obviously old-fashioned and provincial—quite out of the mainstream of life in our advanced civilization of the West. The ethos of an aristocratic governing class exists, in memory at least, along with a vigorous folk culture, a culture of farms and small towns, where personal relationships will be concrete and morally uncomplicated, with very little buffering by abstract entities such as corporate bureaucracies, trade unions, and such. In this society one will have a good idea of who has done him a service and who has done him a hurt. The consequence of this will be a certain level of violence and a definite stress on manners. That is, everyone will take care not to offend unless the offence is deliberate and intentional.

Add to these elements certain historical conditions true for both Ireland and the South—defeat in war, economic stagnation, and a colonial economy—and one finds as a consequence that history is very much alive in the minds of the people, for the

dead lost causes are precisely those that live in memory. Yeats
saw the Irish as good haters. In one of his late poems he was still
writing about "The Curse of Cromwell," and in another he says:

> Out of Ireland have we come.
> Great hatred, little room,
> Maimed us at the start.
> I carry from my mother's womb
> A fanatic heart.[19]

Southerners have also proved to be good rememberers—and
sometimes good haters. But if there are risks, there are also values
in being unable to forget one's past history. Faulkner wrote to
Malcolm Cowley that the only "clean thing about War [is]
losing it,"[20] and the context in which he makes this rather cryptic
statement suggests that he meant that a lost war continues to
feed the imagination. C. Vann Woodward makes the point with a
different inflection. In his *Burden of Southern History*, he observes that past defeat begets realism.[21] It tends to inoculate a
culture against the perils of futurism, the pursuit of an ever-
receding Utopia. Wisdom itself may be said to reside in a lively
sense of history. But it is not my aim to argue that it is better for
a country to be poor and proud, provincial and old-fashioned.
Ireland and the American South have both paid dearly for such
not unmixed blessings.

What I am concerned to say is that the kind of cultural situation into which Yeats and Faulkner were born yielded material
which, when seized upon by genius, could be shaped into very
great poetry and fiction.

There are a multitude of ways in which the resources of a
traditional culture could be drawn upon by these two writers.
I must therefore select only a few further examples. Here is a
simple but very important example with reference to style. To
both men there was available an oral tradition—a fountain of
living speech. The Irish like to talk: storytelling and political
oratory are their special delight. Joyce's *Ulysses* is made of such
talk, ranging from an admiring recital of John F. Taylor's famous oration on the Irish language to the witty give and take of

two raconteurs in a pub. Southerners also like to talk. Southern oratory is now considerably frayed, but Senator Ervin, as people who heard him in the Watergate hearings can testify, could still produce the authentic ring, and the art of telling a tale is still very much alive. Andrew Lytle, for example, is a living master of this style that comes down from hunters around a campfire or a group chatting on the porch of a country store.

In 1937 Yeats, in one of his latest pieces of prose, talked about the importance to him of this oral tradition. He says: "I have spent my life in clearing out of poetry every phrase written for the eye, and bringing all back to syntax that is for ear alone." This is surely part of the secret of the great sinewy style of his later poetry—the poetry that by 1914 was beginning to replace the languid, dreamy verse of his earliest period and the mannered prose of "The Tables of the Law." Let me repeat Yeats's wonderful phrase: "bringing all back to syntax that is for ear alone."[22] Could there be a better description of Faulkner's prose?

I shall not undertake to give examples of what I mean. I doubt that there is any need to provide examples to this particular audience. I need only recall to you such passages as Jason's furious monologue in *The Sound and the Fury*, or Miss Rosa's frenetic tirade in *Absalom, Absalom!* or the wonderful "Spotted Horses" portion of *The Hamlet*. The ear does indeed rejoice in these passages. Moreover, even Faulkner's long, involved sentences, the syntax of which sometimes seems impossibly tangled, straighten themselves out when read aloud—perhaps only when read aloud.

I have alluded to Yeats's celebrated change in style. But Faulkner changed his style too, in moving from poetry to prose, and, in doing so, effected a radical shift of the same order. For Faulkner's formal verse is dreamy and romantic in much the same way as is Yeats's early poetry and indeed consciously imitates it and the poetry of Yeats's friends and companions of the period. Faulkner always spoke of himself as a failed poet: he could not write the poetry he wanted to write, he tells us, and so turned to prose. But what a fortunate failure. Moreover, how quickly, as compared with Yeats, did Faulkner sense the need for a new direction and take it. Indeed, if we date Yeats's great alteration of style to about 1914, it is worth noting that Faulkner, though 34 years younger, had set his feet on his proper course only a dozen years later than had Yeats himself.

I wish that I had time to develop the significance in the change, for it was of crucial significance in both instances. Both writers were coming out of their more limited provincial cultures to confront modernity. Perhaps Pound deserves most credit for bringing Yeats to the confrontation; one might argue that it was principally Eliot and Joyce who, not personally, but in their writings, performed a like service for Faulkner. It was not enough that Yeats should continue a minor Irish poet. His local resources became important only as he brought them to bear upon the crucial issues of the twentieth century and so joined the mainstream of international literature. The same should be said of Faulkner. It would have been stupid to praise him as superb local colorist, just as it was stupid to praise him for conducting an alleged exposé of Southern degeneracy. His fiction was not designed either to congratulate or to scold his fellow Southerners. What he succeeded in doing was to use the experience that he knew best in order to interpret universal issues. His cultural heritage proved to be ultimately important in providing him with a special and most valuable perspective on Western civilization as a whole.

One of the universal issues to which his fiction addresses itself is man's relation to nature and to history. Man is clearly a part of nature. When does his departure from nature become a perversion and when a fruitful transcendence? The question arises, for, unlike the other natural creatures, man is able to suspend his natural instinctive drives and break through into the realm of history. Even the wisest of the beasts do not have a proper history. Man does.

Now that we live in a culture that has become more and more ruthless in exploiting nature and more and more contemptuous of the past—and therefore contemptuous of history—man's relation to nature and to history becomes even more important. In a Promethean age, oriented to the future, the past seems dead because nonsignificant. Modern man simply finds it irrelevant.

Yeats and Faulkner found the past alive and meaningful. It was still a living force in Ireland and in the South. The greatest work of both men is suffused with history—not as barren antiquarianism, but as a record of the strivings of man—ultimately unchanging Man—to realize his true self by rising above his habitual self.

There are, however, some significant differences in the role that the two men assign to nature and history. Faulkner addresses himself to nature far more fully than Yeats. Yeats knew the Irish landcape well and he can describe it in loving detail, but his nature is never as immediately impressive as Faulkner's. Faulkner has the more innocent eye for nature and gives himself to it more directly, sometimes veering close to nature worship. One remembers the great hymns to nature in "The Bear " and in *The Hamlet*. In the character of the almost subhuman Ike Snopes, Faulkner describes someone almost as deeply immersed in nature as any animal but not quite. The vital human difference is safeguarded. There is a margin for aesthetic appreciation and even ethical choice. Ike is not just a creature like his beloved cow. He is still recognizably human. In contrast to Faulkner, Yeats never sinks his characters so deep into nature, not even his Crazy Jane or his Tom the Lunatic.

Yet there is one important sense in which Yeats makes history, that specifically human realm, actually subservient to nature. For Yeats, history has no goal; like nature itself, history is not going anywhere. It simply moves through predetermined cycles, of birth, growth, maturity, and decay. Civilizations are like plants that come to flower and fruit in their season, and then suffer their winter of denudation and death. Yeats's favorite metaphor for this process is the waxing and waning of the moon. Our own civilization, he says, lies now under a rapidly darkening moon. In one of his poems he says that passion, whether love or hate, now gives way

> . . . to an indifferent multitude, give[s] place
> To brazen hawks. Nor self-delighting reverie,

Nor hate of what's to come, nor pity for what's gone,
Nothing but grip of claw, and the eye's complacency,
The innumerable clanging wings that have put out the moon.[23]

Naturally, Yeats did not believe in progress, calling it "the sole religious myth of modern man." After all, it was "only two hundred years old."[24] Faulkner evidently did not believe in progress, either, for his Nobel Prize speech does not predict greater triumphs for man in the future but rather insists upon the indestructibility of the human spirit, no matter what the historical vicissitudes that may lie ahead for mankind. Moreover, if I read his fiction aright, there is no more worship of the future than there is of the past. But to return to this matter of nature and history: in spite of Faulkner's love for nature, he saw that the human being has to transcend nature.

Thus, Ike McCaslin learns something very important from his experience of the wilderness: his teacher, Sam Fathers, is a hunter, and he anoints Ike, not with the water from some clear stream or the juice of some wild fruit, but with the hot blood of the slain deer. The choice of blood is significant. Man cannot simply live on nature's freely offered bounty, gathering food from bushes and trees like the unfallen Adam in the Garden of Eden. Man's rupture with nature occurred long ago, and it is irreparable. Man cannot be innocent as an animal is, relying on his own instincts, capable of no "unnatural" action, incapable of moral choice, and thus barred out from the realm of moral good and evil, which is the realm of history and the peculiarly human dimension. Man is compelled to be either better or worse than the beast. He does not live like a bird or a bear in a virtual present, but in the dimension of the past and of the future.

Faulkner, in short, did not believe in the noble savage. The red man who lived for thousands of years in the American wilderness and presumably had learned its laws was not thereby rendered "good." Faulkner is very careful to make clear in "The Bear" that the new world of America was "already tainted even before any white man owned it."[25] It is Ike who is speaking here, but there is little doubt that in this instance he voices Faulkner's own sentiments.

To sum up: man is not naturally good. He must achieve his goodness—even his basic humanity—by discipline and effort. True, he must respect his creaturehood. He must respect nature and the other natural creatures. If he kills deer and bear, he must try to be worthy of the blood that he spills. He must, if this does not sound too much of a contradiction, actually do his killing, not wantonly, but out of respect and love. More is expected of man than of any other creature. He must do much better than nature, lest he do worse. He must therefore live by a discipline and self-imposed code of honor. The history of man is the history of the creation of such codes and man's struggle to live up to them or his failure to do so. Faulkner's heroes struggle mightily to do so. His villains like Flem Snopes or Jason Compson are men who deliberately disavow not only the aristocratic code of the Old South but any fully human code. Flem Snopes is no aristocrat; he is a successful plutocrat; Jason Compson is a failed plutocrat.

Yeats's view of man in relation to nature and history is rather surprisingly like Faulkner's. In his magnificent "Prayer for My Daughter," written in 1919, the poet views with foreboding the stormy future that faces his infant daughter. Yeats proved to be a true prophet: the world-wide Depression, Hitler and the Second World War, the Cold War, and all the other ills of the midcentury lay ahead.

The poet prays that his daughter will be beautiful, but not so beautiful as to have a proud and disdainful heart; that she may be chiefly learned in courtesy; that she may never be filled with intellectual hatred; and that she may recover a radical innocence by coming to know her deepest self. The concluding stanza reads as follows:

> And may her bridegroom bring her to a house
> Where all's accustomed, ceremonious;
> For arrogance and hatred are the wares
> Peddled in the thoroughfares.

How but in custom and in ceremony
Are innocence and beauty born?
Ceremony's a name for the rich horn,
And custom for the spreading laurel tree.[26]

We ordinarily think of innocence and beauty as the free gift
of nature, and we commonly oppose them to custom and ceremony, which we too often dismiss as at best empty formalisms
and at worst as corrupting sophistications; but Yeats has boldly
inverted these relationships. True innocence and beauty, he
declares, are not the produce of nature, but the fruits of a disciplined life. Far from being capriciously given to us, we must
achieve them for ourselves. They are not from nature but from
nurture. To all of which Faulkner's Miss Jenny Du Pre, I have no
doubt, would have uttered a fervent Amen.

I have suggested that the view of man held by both Yeats and
Faulkner is on its positive side aristocratic and heroic. Clearly, if
I am right, it also has close affinities to the orthodox Classical-
Christian view of man, though both men had some very severe
things to say about the institutional Christianity of their times.
Perhaps I can best approach their basic conception of man by
looking at it from the negative side. Faulkner very often implied
his positive view by a scarifying depiction of what was *not* good,
beautiful, or true. *Sanctuary* constitutes an extreme instance.
Horace Benbow learns (and the reader with him perhaps) that
girlish innocence as incarnate in Temple Drake and Little Belle
is not innocent in the least.

Yeats opposed to his heroic idea what he called "Whiggery."
In a poem called "The Seven Sages," seven old Irish grayheads
discuss the Irish past and its eighteenth-century heroes and the
state of the modern world. One of them observes that their heroes
were united in their hatred of Whiggery, and proceeds to define
the hated thing:

. . . what is Whiggery?
A levelling, rancorous, rational sort of mind
That never looked out of the eye of a saint
Or out of a drunkard's eye.[27]

Faulkner never used the term "Whiggery." For him, it would probably have denoted no more than a quite defunct, pre-Civil War political party. But Faulkner knew the thing even though he did not know Yeats's, and T. S. Eliot's, name for it. Who would be some of his "Whigs"?

For an excellent example of the "rancorous, rational sort of mind," what about Jason Compson? He is quite sure that he is practical and reasonable. Let others be sentimental, or enthusiastic, or silly in their emotional excesses. He will be eminently rational. In the Appendix to *The Sound and the Fury*, Faulkner calls him "the first sane Compson since Culloden."[28]

As for the kind of eye through which the mind of Whiggery looks out upon the world, what about Flem Snopes's? Faulkner describes Flem's eye as the color of stagnant water, and the description is telling. Flem lacks the other-worldly rapture of the saint or the drunkard. Ecstasy—being able to stand outside one's self and one's narrow range of interests—that is what is quite impossible for Flem, who is impotent and without appetites of any kind. It is just as hard to imagine him jovially tipsy as it is to imagine him on his knees in prayer.

Thus, I find Yeats and Faulkner, different as they are in a hundred ways, nevertheless very much alike in their vision of modern man in relation to nature and to history. As one looks back on the work of these two great writers, one is inclined to say, "Thank God for their achievements in our time," but it occurs to me that we ought also to thank that same power (or whatever powers we decide to thank) that both were born into cultural milieux that shaped and helped make possible their mighty works.

NOTES

1. *Go Down Moses*, Modern Library Edition, p. 178.
2. Ibid., p. 164.
3. Ibid., pp. 186–87.
4. Ibid., p. 187.
5. W. B. Yeats, *Essays and Introductions* (London: Macmillan,

1961), p. 518.

6. Ibid., p. 518

7. *Go Down, Moses,* pp. 186–87.

8. Ibid., p. 136.

9. Ibid., p. 223.

10. Donald T. Torchiana, *Yeats and Georgian Ireland* (Evanston: Northwestern University Press, 1966), pp. 89–90.

11. *The Faulkner-Cowley File,* ed. Malcolm Cowley (New York: Viking, 1966), p. 66.

12. Torchiana, p. 89.

13. In "There Was a Queen."

14. *Sanctuary* (New York: Random House, 1963), p. 103.

15. Ibid., p. 254.

16. W. B. Yeats, *Collected Poems* (New York: Macmillan, 1955), p. 343.

17. Ibid., p. 107.

18. Ibid., p. 106.

19. Ibid., p. 249.

20. *Faulkner-Cowley File,* p. 79.

21. C. Vann Woodward, *The Burden of Southern History* (Baton Rouge: Louisiana State University Press, 1960), p. 21.

22. *Essays and Introductions,* p. 529.

23. Yeats, *Collected Poems,* pp. 203–04.

24. W. B. Yeats, *Wheels and Butterflies,* (London: Macmillan, 1934), p. 20.

25. *Go Down, Moses,* p. 259.

26. Yeats, *Collected Poems,* p. 187.

27. Ibid., p. 236.

28. Modern Library Edition, p. 420.

# Faulkner's Essays
# on Anderson

The whole subject of William Faulkner's relationship, personal and literary, with Sherwood Anderson is one of very great interest, and also of not a little difficulty and complexity. The two men met in New Orleans in the fall of 1924, not long before the publication of *The Marble Faun*. Faulkner was young and unknown; Anderson, twenty-one years his senior, was a mature and established writer. During the spring of 1925 the two men spent a good deal of time together in New Orleans and became good friends; subsequently they quarreled, and thereafter saw little of each other. Both of them left us more or less fictionalized accounts of their meeting, of their friendship, and of the cause of their quarrel; each has given us at least a brief estimate of the other as a man and as a writer.

Although there are episodes and elements in their relationship that are difficult to assess with any degree of confidence, it is certain that Anderson was an exceptionally important formative influence on Faulkner. Indeed, there is only one other influence, that of his earlier friend and mentor Phil Stone, that had a comparable effect upon Faulkner's career—and it is significant that Faulkner himself, in the period after he had become established as a writer, repeatedly acknowledged the importance of Anderson's role in his development but said almost nothing about Stone.

Much has already been written about the Faulkner-Anderson relationship. The friendship of the two men has been chronicled by several distinguished Faulkner scholars: first and most notably

159

by Carvel Collins, in the introduction to his edition of Faulkner's *New Orleans Sketches*; then by Michael Millgate, who added significantly to Collins' picture of the two in the biographical chapter of his *Achievement of William Faulkner*; and most recently by Joseph Blotner, in his massively useful recent two-volume *Faulkner: A Biography*. We can look forward to further information from Collins in his long-awaited biography of Faulkner; and I am sure that a great deal more light will be shed upon this complex and fascinating personal and literary relationship when Walter Rideout's biography of Anderson is published.[1]

I make no claims for myself as a biographer of Faulkner, and there is very little that I can add to what has already been said about the facts of the Faulkner-Anderson relationship by these distinguished literary biographers. Nor do I speak as a literary historian, though Richard P. Adams and Thomas L. McHaney, especially, have shown the significance of Faulkner's use, in his fiction, of material he took both from Anderson's life and from his work, and though it is clear that further investigations along such lines could prove very useful.[2]

Instead, I speak here primarily as a literary critic, and I deal only with two texts, neither of them fiction (although at least one of them is largely fictional in its method). These are the two essays that Faulkner wrote on Anderson, one very early in his career, the other late. They have received relatively little attention, and yet they can tell us a great deal about Faulkner, if not about Anderson. What I should like to do here, then, is to offer an analysis and interpretation of these two brief but highly significant pieces, one written in 1925, the other in 1953, in the hope that by examining them in somewhat greater detail and from a somewhat different viewpoint than has been attempted before, I can shed a little more light upon them, and upon their difficult and occasionally enigmatic author, William Faulkner.

The earlier of these essays was written during the first two or three weeks of April 1925 and was published in the Dallas *Morning News* on Sunday, April 26. On March 30, the literary editor of the *Morning News*, John McGinnis, had written his friend John McClure, who held the same position with the New

Orleans *Times-Picayune*, asking him if he would contribute an article on Anderson for a series on modern American authors that was appearing in the *Morning News*. (The series had begun with an article on Sinclair Lewis by a professor at the University of Texas that in McGinnis's opinion had been a little too academic.)

McClure turned down the request but suggested that Faulkner be given the assignment instead. McGinnis must have agreed; he received the piece on April 21 and wrote McClure the same day to say that though he found it too long, Faulkner's essay was "interesting and pertinent throughout." After it appeared, he again wrote McClure to say that he hoped the check had arrived (Faulkner would have received ten dollars, five dollars per column) and that he had run the essay "with little cutting."[3]

As published, the essay begins with some brief comments on various theories concerning Anderson's literary sources—which are rather offhandedly dismissed by Faulkner: "For some reason people seem to be interested not in what Mr. Anderson has written, but from what source he derives."[4] After rejecting the suggestion of French and Russian sources, Faulkner continues, "Like most speculation all this is interesting but bootless. Men grow from the soil, like corn and trees: I prefer to think of Mr. Anderson as a lusty corn field in his native Ohio." (Unfortunately this somewhat strained agricultural image for Anderson and his work is tediously elaborated and extended by the young critic through the rest of the essay.)

Faulkner then proceeds to give brief analyses of seven of Anderson's books—seven out of the total of nine that he had published between 1916 and 1924. The two books omitted are *Mid-American Chants*, a book of verse published in 1918; and, curiously, *The Triumph of the Egg*, Anderson's fine 1921 collection of stories. One wonders if Faulkner's comments on them were cut out by McGinnis; *Mid-American Chants* is unimportant Anderson (though it might be interesting to know what Faulkner thought of it, since his own one published book was verse), but *The Triumph of the Egg* is another matter. Later on Faulkner certainly knew it—he praised it as one of Anderson's three best books in his 1953 essay—and it is most unlikely that he would have taken the trouble to read Anderson's early novels while ignoring a fine recent collection of stories.

Whatever the reason for omitting *Mid-American Chants* and *The Triumph of the Egg*, Faulkner's brief comments on the others show that he had read them carefully and arrived at decided opinions concerning them—opinions that offer interesting and occasionally illuminating criticism of Anderson, and opinions that also tell us a good deal about William Faulkner, a young author who was himself engaged in the writing of his first novel.

He begins with *Winesburg, Ohio*, praising it highly, but making one very interesting error, or false assumption, about it. He thinks it is Anderson's first book (published in 1919, it was actually his fourth), and he makes the patronizing and revealing comment, "As a rule first books show more bravado than anything else, unless it be tediousness. But there is neither of these qualities in 'Winesburg.' "

Faulkner praises the book for its characterization—"These people live and breathe"—though he has reservations about Anderson's attitude toward his creations: his sympathy for the fictional characters of the book, to Faulkner's mind, "would have become mawkish" if the work had been "a full-length novel."

The comment is interesting in more ways than one. Clearly Faulkner did not consider that the work possessed the structure of a novel—he had begun with praise for Anderson because the "stories" of the book "are as simply done: short, he tells the story and stops." Faulkner, that spring, was busy writing short stories as well as his first novel, and he had reason to be particularly aware of the difficulties he might encounter in the deeper and more elaborate characterizations of the novel if he carried over into it some of the attitudes and narrative methods he was using in the short fictional sketches he had begun contributing to the New Orleans *Times-Picayune* in February and in such longer stories as the still unpublished "Peter" and "Don Giovanni" that he was working on at about the same time.[5] In his early novels

Faulkner's interest in his characters was hardly aloof or detached; he showed concern, even passionate concern, for their motives and their fates. But Faulkner also displayed little of the warm and brooding love for his creations that Anderson so often showed, and his scornful use of the term "mawkish" here reveals his already well-developed distrust of sentiment not kept in tight control.

The next four books Faulkner comments on are novels, the only four Anderson had written by then. *Windy McPherson's Son* and *Marching Men*—Anderson's first two books (1916 and 1917), though Faulkner obviously thinks that they follow *Winesburg*—are dismissed in a few sentences each. Both are hurt by "a fundamental lack of humor," Faulkner thinks. On the other hand, for *Poor White* (1920) Faulkner has high praise. "In this book," he says, Anderson "seems to get his fingers and toes again into the soil, as he did in 'Winesburg,' " and again creates characters "who answer the compulsions of labor and food and sleep, whose passions are uncerebral." But in *Many Marriages* (1922) Anderson "gets away from the land"; when he does this, "he is lost. And again humor is completely lacking."

The final two critical sketches of the essay are also the longest and the most interesting. They deal with the collection *Horses and Men* (1923) and with the part-autobiographical, part-fictional *A Story-Teller's Story* (1924). The former Faulkner calls "reminiscent of 'Winesburg,' but more sophisticated," and he wonders "if after all the short story is not Mr. Anderson's medium. No sustained plot to bother you . . . only the sharp episodic phases of people, the portraying of which Mr. Anderson's halting questioning manner is best at." He notes especially "I'm a Fool," calling it "the best short story in America, to my thinking," and concludes with an apostrophe to the horse, its place in history and its relationship to man, which anticipates, in its tone of humorously overblown rhetoric, the well-known apostrophe to the mule which Faulkner would include two years later in his own novel *Flags in the Dust*.[6]

His comments on *A Story-Teller's Story* are significant for what Faulkner says about Anderson's mingling of fact and fiction, his use of autobiographical material, and the function of humor. In this work, says Faulkner, Anderson, in

> trying to do one thing, has really written two distinct books. The first half, which was evidently intended to portray his physical picture, is really a novel based upon one character—his father. . . . The second half of the book in which he draws his mental portrait is quite different: it leaves me with a faint feeling that it should have been in a separate volume.
>
> Here Mr. Anderson pries into his own mind. . . . Up to here he is never philosophical; he believes that he knows little about it all, and leaves the reader to draw his own conclusions. He does not even offer opinions.
>
> But in this second half of the book he assumes at times an elephantine kind of humor about himself, not at all the keen humor with which he pictured his father's character. I think that this is due to the fact that Mr. Anderson is interested in his reactions to other people, and very little in himself. That is, he has not enough active ego to write successfully of himself.

And Faulkner elaborates the point that lack of humor has affected Anderson's perspective, his handling of character in his fiction:

> I do not mean to imply that Mr. Anderson has no sense of humor. He has, he has always had. But only recently has he got any of it into his stories, without deliberately writing a story with a humorous intent. I wonder sometimes if this is not due to the fact that he didn't have leisure to write until long after these people had come to be in his mind; that he had cherished them until his perspective was slightly awry. . . .

On the other hand, no one, continues Faulkner, "can accuse him of lacking in humor in the portrayal of the father" in *A Story-Teller's Story*. And with regrettable condescension Faulkner adds, "which, I think, indicates that he has not matured yet. . . ."

Faulkner concludes his little essay by recounting an anecdote that he says Anderson told him:

> We were spending a week-end on a river boat, Anderson

and I. I had not slept much and so I was out and watching the sun rise, turning the muddy reaches of the Mississippi even, temporarily to magic, when he joined me, laughing.

"I had a funny dream last night. Let me tell you about it," was his opening remark—not even a good morning.

"I dreamed that I couldn't sleep, that I was riding around the country on a horse—had ridden for days. At last I met a man, and I swapped him the horse for a night's sleep. This was in the morning and he told me where to bring the horse, and so when dark came I was right on time, standing in front of his house, holding the horse, ready to rush off to bed. But the fellow never showed up—left me standing there all night, holding the horse."

As Faulkner tells it here—or as he here gives Anderson credit for telling it—this pleasantly humorous dream-anecdote clearly has more than a little symbolic potential. It fairly cries out for interpretation; but Faulkner gives none. Perhaps an editorial cut was responsible. Since Faulkner offers another version of it in his 1953 essay, and on that occasion supplies a highly enlightening interpretation, I am inclined to blame McGinnis for the awkward lack of comment on it here.[7]

The 1925 essay has quite a few faults—the awkward attempt to develop the image of Anderson as a cornfield is one (*Many Marriages*, for example, is called "a bad ear" and of the humorless *Windy McPherson's Son* it is said that "growing corn has little time for humor"). Another blunder, which leads to a faulty picture of Anderson's development as an artist, is the misdating of *Winesburg*. And I think Faulkner can be fairly accused of uncertainty in tone, and even lapses of taste, from time to time. But these are the faults of youth, and Faulkner shows real strengths and virtues in the essay, too. The piece is clearly the work of someone who knows Anderson personally and likes him, who has read most of Anderson's books with an appreciative but critical eye, and who has no hesitation in speaking his mind about both the author and his work. The essay shows knowledge of what other critics have written about Anderson and deals succinctly with a number of general trends in literary criticism as they affect Anderson. Knowing nothing else about Faulkner, one could still judge from the piece that its author, if young, was also intelligent, serious, and self-confident in his literary judgments. One might also guess that he had a particular interest in the problems of using autobiographical material in fiction, in the necessity for an organic relationship between an author's native place and his work, and in the function of humor in the establishment of narrative perspective and fictional characterization.

In my opening remarks, I referred to Faulkner's 1953 essay as his second on Sherwood Anderson. However, it would be more precise to call it his third, for there is evidence that he wrote another, which he attempted to publish in 1927. Unfortunately, it appears not to have survived. On August 16, 1927, Phil Stone sent the article by Faulkner to the *New Republic*, of which their friend Stark Young was an editor. Because Stone reveals knowledge and opinions that he obviously shared with Faulkner—at least the Faulkner of the 1925 essay—as well as a good deal of himself, his accompanying letter deserves to be quoted in its entirety:

> I have just read in the New Republic for August 3rd Lawrence Morris' article on Sherwood Anderson. While I think part of it is accurate I think the two great troubles with Anderson are mere garrulity and a lack of a sense of humor. Mr. William Falkner of this place was associated with Mr. Anderson for a good part of a year and has written an article on Anderson which I am sending you under separate cover and am submitting it at your usual rates. It seems to me that this article has much more insight than the one by Morris.
>
> Mr. Falkner is the author of "Soldiers' Pay" and "Mosquitoes" both published by Boni & Liverright. In fact Mr. Anderson is the prototype for the character of Dawson Fairchild in "Mosquitoes".
>
> If you care to use this article send check to William Falkner, University, Mississippi.

The essay was not published by the *New Republic*, however. On November 21, 1927, Stone wrote again, repeating some of his comments from the earlier letter and requesting that the manuscript be returned—apparently it had been rejected.[8] Should this lost essay turn up, it would be extraordinarily interesting to see if, and in what way, Faulkner's opinions of Anderson had changed in the intervening two years. We may recall that in September 1927 Faulkner had completed the writing of *Flags in the Dust*, which two years later would be published, under the title of *Sartoris*, with a moving dedication to Anderson. It is pleasant to speculate that perhaps in this essay Faulkner tried to make amends for the brashness of his 1925 criticism—at least for its implied condescension. (Carvel Collins has suggested that the earlier essay was brought to Anderson's attention and played a part in the break between the two men.[9]) But the chances of its turning up again now seem slight, and so we can only speculate.

To turn from the 1925 to the 1953 essay is to turn from awkward, if interesting, apprentice work to the profound and deeply moving product of artistic maturity. "A Note on Sherwood Anderson" was written in February 1953, apparently commissioned by the editor of *The Atlantic Monthly* as an introduction to a group of Anderson's letters which they were to publish.[10] What they got was not the introduction they wanted; instead they got one of the finest and most important essays that Faulkner ever wrote—in my opinion, one of his two best literary essays, along with the 1933 introduction he wrote for *The Sound and the Fury*. And like that essay, but even more like the semi-autobiographical "Mississippi," which he also wrote in 1953, "A Note on Sherwood Anderson" is also a profoundly moving and significant personal document.

For the subject—the real subject—of the 1953 Anderson essay is not Sherwood Anderson, or even Faulkner's relationship with Anderson, but rather Faulkner's experience, at about the time he knew Anderson, of growing up as a young writer, of entering upon his career as a novelist. By this I do not mean to imply that the essay is essentially autobiographical, although what it says, I have no doubt, is very true of William Faulkner the young man, the young artist, at approximately this point in his career. But the essay is, I am sure, *true* only in the sense that Faulkner liked to use the term, when he distinguished *truth* from *fact*. And I think it would be a serious error to read this essay in search of any actual facts of the Anderson-Faulkner relationship.[11] In many ways this is less an essay than a parable, a parable of the relationship of a young writer to an older one, or of an apprentice finding himself, learning his art and craft through the precept and example of a master. And Faulkner from the beginning gives the reader an invitation—an uncharacteristically obvious invitation—to interpret what he says here as a parable and to seek his essential meaning well beneath the surface of his story.

For he begins the piece with another telling—expanded and enriched—of Anderson's tale of swapping a horse for a night's sleep:

> One day during the months while we walked and talked in New Orleans—or Anderson talked and I listened—I found him sitting on a bench in Jackson Square, laughing with himself. I got the impression that he had been there like that for some time, just sitting alone on the bench laughing with himself. . . . He told me what it was at once: a dream: he had dreamed the night before that he was walking for miles along country roads, leading a horse which he was trying to swap for a night's sleep —not for a simple bed for the night, but for the sleep itself; and with me to listen now, went on from there, elaborating it, building it into a work of art with the same tedious (it had the appearance of fumbling but actually it wasn't; it was seeking, hunting) almost excruciating patience and humility with which he did all his writing, me listening and believing no word of it: that is, that it had been any dream dreamed in sleep. Because I knew better. I knew that he had invented it, made it; he had made most of it or at least some of it while I was there watching and listening to him. He didn't know why he had been compelled, or anyway needed, to claim it had been a dream, why there had to be that connection with dream and sleep, but I did. It was because he had written his whole biography into an anecdote or perhaps a parable: the horse . . . representing the vast rich strong docile sweep of the Mississippi Valley, his own America, which he . . . was offering with humor and patience and humility, but mostly with patience and humility, to swap for his own dream of purity and integrity and hard and unremitting work

and accomplishment, of which *Winesburg, Ohio* and *The Triumph of the Egg* had been symptoms and symbols.[12]

This telling by Faulkner of Anderson's dream, with Faulkner's own highly condensed explication of it, invites further explication by the reader. It also invites comparison with other works by Faulkner in which he is concerned with the same themes and materials. For example, it may remind us more than a little of the early short story "Carcassonne," which is likewise a parable of the artist's life and uses the same devices of the horse and the dream, though in more complex fashion—and no one has yet given "Carcassonne" its due as a deliberate attempt on Faulkner's part to embody, in a short piece of symbolic fiction, his artistic ideals and ambitions.[13] This occasion is not one upon which to embark on a lengthy explication of what Faulkner, in Anderson's name, may be doing here with that dream, that horse, and that night's sleep. But it is worth pointing out here some of the major points that Faulkner must have been trying to make when he used this anecdote, and his comments on it, to begin his essay on Anderson.

We might note first that Faulkner, somewhat surprisingly, says that though Anderson himself might not have known what he was doing, he, Faulkner, "knew better"—knew what Anderson didn't know; knew why Anderson had had to claim that it had been a dream, why there had to be a connection between dream and sleep. But Faulkner knew, and the reason was that Anderson "had written his whole biography" into the parable. In short, Anderson had to tell the story of his life, had done so in the form of a parable, had been "compelled" to mask it as a dream—and Faulkner had understood what it all meant.

If we follow Faulkner's explication a little further, though, knotty problems appear. Anderson dreamed, or spoke, of himself, sleepless, walking for miles, and leading a horse that he wanted to swap for a night's sleep. In Faulkner's interpretation, the horse represented Anderson's America—midwestern America, the Mississippi Valley—which Anderson was trying to swap for—that is, was willing to get rid of in exchange for—the sleep, which Faulkner says represents Anderson's dream as an artist

—his "dream of purity and integrity and hard and unremitting work and accomplishment." It sounds, at first, as if Anderson were giving up his artistic heritage, or materials—his real subject matter—in exchange for release, relief from reality, from daylight life. In short, it sounds a little as if the strain of that dedication to his art, that "hard and unremitting work," were too much, or almost too much, for Anderson, and that he chose this means of revealing the fact.

But Faulkner's interpretation invites a somewhat different, or deeper, reading. Anderson wants the sleep—wants the dream-world, the world beyond ordinary reality, symbolized by the dream itself he claims to be describing—a dream that Faulkner has already said is not a dream, but a deliberate, created work of art made by Anderson to communicate to Faulkner. Anderson longs for this world of art, of the artist, and makes the symbolic artist's journey to it, walking those miles down country roads—and all he has to offer for it, all that might enable him to attain it, is his mid-America, his strong, rich Mississippi Valley heritage. The "swap" is conversion; in order to attain his goal, the ideal, Anderson had to begin with the actual—and be willing to use it and even to give it up.

Faulkner goes on, then, to explain further why Anderson himself would not or could not have interpreted his own parable in such fashion:

> He would never have said this, put it into words, himself. He may never have been able to see it even, and he certainly would have denied it, probably pretty violently, if I had tried to point it out to him. But this would not have been for the reason that it might not have been true, nor for the reason that, true or not, he would not have believed it. In fact, it would have made little difference whether it was true or not or whether he believed it or not. He would have repudiated it for the reason which was the great tragedy of his character. He expected people to make fun of, ridicule him. He expected people nowhere near his equal in stature or accomplishment or wit or anything else, to be capable of making him appear ridiculous.

It is interesting to find here Faulkner apparently arguing the critic's side against that of the writer—upholding the validity of his own interpretation of Anderson's art, even though the man himself, the artist, would have denied it. But Faulkner's real point lies further on; his concern is to show *why* Anderson could not accept the truth that Faulkner could discern in his parable. And this carries him to a discussion of Anderson's style —or of Anderson's attitude, as an artist, toward style.

This is the reason why Anderson, according to Faulkner,

> . . . worked so laboriously and tediously and indefatigably at everything he wrote. It was as if he said to himself: "This anyway, will, shall, must be invulnerable." It was as though he wrote not even out of the consuming unsleeping appeaseless thirst for glory for which any normal artist would destroy his aged mother, but for what to him was more important and urgent: not even for mere truth, but for purity, the exactitude of purity. His was not the power and rush of Melville, who was his grandfather, nor the lusty humor for living of Twain, who was his father; he had nothing of the heavy-handed disregard for nuances of his older brother, Dreiser. His was that fumbling for exactitude, the exact word and phrase within the limited scope of a vocabulary controlled and even repressed by what was in him almost a fetish of simplicity, to milk them both dry, to seek always to penetrate to thought's uttermost end. He worked so hard at this that it finally became just style: an end instead of a means: so that he presently came to believe that, provided he kept the style pure and intact and unchanged and inviolate, what the style contained would have to be first rate: it couldn't help but be first rate, and therefore himself too.

Anderson's great flaw, then, was to confuse means with end; to make style, not content, his main object in writing; to pursue too far the goal of purity and exactitude—leading to the loss of those qualities that Faulkner had praised in those other American novelists. Power and rush, lusty humor for living, even a "heavy-handed disregard for nuances," it would seem, are better than what Anderson sought, or finally achieved.

Faulkner had made the same point in 1941, when in a letter to Warren Beck he emphasized his own decision not to concern himself too much with stylistic niceties. "As yet I have found no happy balance between method and material," he wrote Beck.

> I doubt that it exists for me. . . . I decided what seems to me now a long time ago that something worth saying knew better than I did how it needed to be said, and that it was better said poorly even than not said. . . . I discovered then that I had rather read Shakespeare, bad puns, bad history, taste and all, than Pater, and that I had a damn sight rather fail at trying to write Shakespeare than to write all of Pater over again so he couldn't have told it himself if you fired it point blank at him through an amplifier.[14]

Neither Faulkner's humor nor his modesty should mislead us; we know from the many surviving and carefully revised manuscript and typescript drafts of his works that Faulkner labored hard and devotedly to improve his writing, down to and including the most minute details of punctuation and word arrangement. But it is equally clear that he must have made up his mind, very early, not to polish and refine his style to the point that it would lose its vitality. And I see no reason to doubt the general truth of his assertion here, that he learned this lesson at the beginning of his career as a novelist, and that he learned it, at least in part, from Anderson.

Faulkner then goes on to tell the story of how he had hurt Anderson by parodying his style in his introduction to the little booklet of caricatures, *Sherwood Anderson & Other Famous Creoles* (1926), which leads to an interesting comment on Anderson himself:

> He was a sentimentalist in his attitude toward people, and quite often incorrect about them. He believed in people, but it was as though only in theory. He expected the worst from them, even while each time he was prepared again to be disappointed or even hurt, as if it had never happened before, as though the only people he could really trust, let himself go with, were the ones of his own invention, the figments and symbols of his own fumbling dream.

Such a criticism, of course, implies that the critic making the judgment—that is, Faulkner—lacks the weakness being criticized. And I think that this is true—both in his life and in his writings, Faulkner clearly revealed a greater strength and toughness than Anderson, a less sentimental attitude toward people, and better judgment of his fellow human beings. Faulkner's objectivity about both Anderson and himself, here, is noteworthy: he is neither praising Faulkner nor condemning Anderson, but discussing the demands that art makes of her practitioners, pointing out the dangers of sentimentalizing the real world and, hence, of trusting too much the world of the imagination.

At this point in his essay, Faulkner gives us the story of his collaboration with Anderson in the invention of the mythical Al Jackson and his family—the same combination of a gesture of friendship with a literary exercise that he was to engage in with Phil Stone a little later on, in the creation of the Snopes tribe.

> During those afternoons when we would walk about the old quarter . . . or the evenings while we sat somewhere over a bottle, he, with a little help from me, invented other fantastic characters like the sleepless man with the horse. One of them was supposed to be a descendant of Andrew Jackson, left in that Louisiana swamp after the Battle of Chalmette, no longer half-horse half-alligator but by now half-man half-sheep and presently half-shark, who—it, the whole fable—at last got so unwieldy and (so we thought) so funny, that we decided to get it onto paper by writing letters to one another such as two temporarily separated members of an exploring-zoological expedition might.

The point of the story, as Faulkner tells it, is what Anderson tried to teach him about the necessity of striving for perfection even in something done so informally and privately. For Anderson

> hated glibness; if it were quick, he believed it was false too. He told me once: "You've got too much talent. You can do it too easy, in too many different ways. If you're not careful, you'll never write anything."

So, Faulkner continues,

> I brought him my first reply to his first letter. He read it. He said:
> "Does it satisfy you?"
> I said, "Sir?"
> "Are you satisfied with it?"
> "Why not?" I said. "I'll put whatever I left out into the next one." Then I realised that he was more than displeased: he was short, stern, almost angry. He said:
> "Either throw it away, and we'll quit, or take it back and do it over." I took the letter. I worked three days over it before I carried it back to him. He read it again, quite slowly, as he always did, and said, "Are you satisfied now?"
> "No sir," I said. "But it's the best I know how to do."
> "Then we'll pass it," he said, putting the letter into his pocket, his voice once more warm, rich, burly with laughter, ready to believe, ready to be hurt again.

After this engaging account of Anderson's using the Al Jackson letters to teach him the necessity for a craftsman to avoid the glib and the sloppy, always to revise and perfect, Faulkner turns to another lesson, one that concerns the artist rather than the craftsman and one that, though I have considerable doubt that it was taught to Faulkner by Anderson, I have no doubt at all in calling one of the most important lessons that Faulkner ever learned. From Anderson, Faulkner says,

> I learned that, to be a writer, one has first got to be what he is, what he was born; that to be an American and a writer, one does not necessarily have to pay lip-service to any conventional American image such as his and Dreiser's own aching Indiana or Ohio or Iowa corn or Sandburg's stockyards or Mark Twain's frog. You had only to remember what you were. "You have to have somewhere to start from: then you begin to learn," he told me. "It dont matter where it was, just so you remember it and aint ashamed of it. Because one place to start from is just as important as any other. You're a country boy; all you know is that little patch up there in Mississippi where you started from."

One reason for doubting that Anderson should receive all the credit for this great lesson is that before he went to New Orleans and became Anderson's friend, Faulkner had clearly already made up his mind to settle down in his native place and to make "that little patch up there in Mississippi," where he had started from, the center of his life and of his work. Both in the poem "Mississippi Hills: My Epitaph," which he wrote in the fall of 1924, and in the essay "Verse Old and Nascent: A Pilgrimage," which he published soon afterward,[15] Faulkner made it clear that he already had made this decision. So it may be that Anderson is here getting credit that belongs at least in part to Phil Stone; and we may well suppose Faulkner to have been capable of learning the lesson on his own. Perhaps one reason that Faulkner associates the lesson with Anderson is that Stone had wanted him to be a poet, while it was under Anderson's influence that he turned decisively to the writing of fiction. Stone had done his best to persuade the young poet to settle down and make his native place the center of his life, but it is to Anderson that Faulkner gives final credit for showing him that it should also be the center of his work.[16]

Let me now emphasize what seems to me a key phrase in Faulkner's account of his learning this great lesson:

> It dont matter where it was, just so you
> remember it and aint ashamed of it.

What could be simpler, or more important? This too, may be a lesson that Phil Stone should share credit for teaching to Faulkner—or that Faulkner himself should take a major share of the credit for learning. I assume that in making this statement (or crediting Anderson with making it) Faulkner was showing his awareness that certain of his critics believed that he was "ashamed" of his native place—perhaps because they themselves thought that he ought to be ashamed of it. But there is no evidence that Faulkner was ashamed of it in the sense he is using the word here, any more than he would have been ashamed of the faults and weaknesses of any other part of the earth that was his. (That some of his characters had such guilt feelings is another matter.) And there is abundant evidence that he felt that his "little patch" of Mississippi soil was "just as important as any other"; whether he learned it from Anderson or not, it was an essential lesson, and he had to learn it at least as early as the beginning of his career as a novelist. As an artist, as a writer, and particularly as a Southern writer, this lesson was vital to his health, to his strength, and to his capacity for growth. His learning it involved a whole complex web of influences and traditions, including what material he could use, what literary techniques he could employ, and what attitudes would govern his relationship with his publishers, his critics, and his readers. These problems had been Anderson's too, and it is clear that Faulkner found much in common with Anderson as a "regional" writer: even though Anderson was not a Southerner, he and Faulkner joined in feeling that they differed in common, and essential, ways from Easterners.

Nevertheless, it seems highly probable that Anderson's attitude toward Faulkner's native South was a factor in their quarrel. Anderson, in his own 1931 essay, "They Come Bearing Gifts," indicates as much, although what he says here about Faulkner probably calls for as much reading between the lines as does Faulkner's 1953 essay on Anderson.[17] Anderson was much attracted by the South, at least partly in reaction to the increasing urbanization and industrialization of the rest of the country. And his Winesburg, Ohio, obviously has much in common with Faulkner's Jefferson, Mississippi. But a major difference between the two writers was that Anderson left his native Midwest, looking for something that he was never to find again, though he found part of it in the South; while Faulkner, though he traveled widely and often, was able to live and work at home. What influence Anderson had it is impossible to determine with exactitude; but it is tempting to follow Faulkner's lead and grant him credit for giving Faulkner some excellent advice—and perhaps also serving as an important negative example.

After his account of what I have called here the "great lesson," Faulkner concludes his essay quietly, with a page or two of more personal summary and final commentary. He praises Anderson the man—"He was warm, generous . . . without pettiness"—and goes on to describe his way of devoting the mornings to writing, then walking around town in the afternoons, and spending his evenings with bottles and good conversation. He tells again the apocryphal story of Anderson agreeing to recommend *Soldiers' Pay* to his own publisher if he, Anderson, wouldn't have to read it. And he concludes with an attempt to focus the essay on Anderson himself, on his fine qualities and the fine work he did, calling him "a giant in an earth populated to a great—too great—extent by pygmies, even if he did make but the two or perhaps three gestures commensurate with gianthood."

But the real meaning of the essay had already been rendered; Anderson was its occasion but not its real subject. Despite the modesty and generosity that characterize Faulkner's account of his being taught certain lessons by Anderson, the significance of what he tells us here lies not so much in what Sherwood Anderson taught, but in what William Faulkner learned.

So rich, so profound, and so deceptively simple-seeming is Faulkner's essay that I feel that I have only touched lightly upon a few of its more obvious points. I suspect that Faulkner, at this point in his career, had very much in mind the question of what a young writer can learn from an older one—or what an older writer can teach a young one. A little more than two years earlier, he had used the occasion of the award of the Nobel Prize to state his creed as a writer, to reveal something of the sources of his belief in his role as an artist. In doing so, he had chosen to address "the young men and women already dedicated to the same anguish and travail"[18]—that is, he was speaking to those young writers all over the world who, as he was becoming increasingly aware, looked up to him as exemplifying the highest of artistic and professional standards. Again, in the essay on Anderson, I am inclined to think, Faulkner was using the commission from the *Atlantic* as an excuse to set forth in print, for whatever audience the occasion provided, something highly important for him to say, as an artist. In effect, I think he used the invitation to write something on Anderson as an opportunity to say just how he had become the artist who was awarded that Nobel Prize—what lessons he had to learn, what weaknesses he had to overcome, what commitments he had to make.

A comment Faulkner made four years later, to an audience at the University of Virginia, serves to support the reading of this essay as primarily an account of what Faulkner had learned, rather than what Anderson taught him. To the question, "Mr. Faulkner, do you think that a writer can teach young writers?" his reply was direct and to the point:

> I don't think anybody can teach anybody anything. I think that you learn it, but the young writer that is . . . demon driven and wants to learn . . . will learn from almost any source that he finds. He will learn from older people who are not writers, he will learn from writers, but he learns it—you can't teach it.[19]

If I am right in thinking that in this essay Faulkner was more concerned to instruct young writers in the principles of their art, as he had been in the Nobel Prize address, than to give an exact account of what he had been taught by Sherwood Anderson; and was more interested in using his early experiences with Anderson as the material for a truthful but unfactual self-portrait of his own development as an artist, as he did in the semifictional "Mississippi," rather than as the basis for an accurate account of their relationship, I fear that it will seem to be one of my points, in my interpretation of the essay, to cut down Anderson's stature by denying him the significance in Faulkner's career that a more literal reading of Faulkner's essay would permit. I would regret this, for it is clear that in this essay, whatever its other purposes may have been, Faulkner was concerned to express his debt to Anderson the man and writer, and his admiration for at least part of Anderson's work.

But I think the essay can sustain the interpretation I have suggested and still remain undiminished in its high praise for an artist whom Faulkner took to be underrated and neglected. In the essay Faulkner emphasizes Anderson's generosity; and the essay also serves to record that quality in Faulkner himself. In effect Faulkner, a proud artist with a very accurate notion of the worth of his own achievement, paid Anderson the highest compliment in his power to bestow, when in this warm and generous tribute he gave Anderson the credit for teaching him, when young, those lessons that his subsequent career had proved he learned so well.

NOTES

1. Carvel Collins, ed., *William Faulkner: New Orleans Sketches* (New York: Random House, 1968). Michael Millgate, *The Achievement of William Faulkner* (New York: Random House, 1966). Joseph Blotner, *Faulkner: A Biography* (New York: Random House, 1974), 2 vols. Collins' biography of Faulkner is scheduled for early publication by Farrar, Straus and Giroux; Rideout's of Anderson, by Oxford University Press.

2. Richard P. Adams, "The Apprenticeship of William Faulkner," *Tulane Studies in English*, 12 (1962), 113–56 (esp. 123–29). Thomas L. McHaney, "Anderson, Hemingway, and Faulkner's *The Wild Palms*," *PMLA*, 87 (1972), 465–74.

3. Carbon copies of McGinnis's letters to McClure of March 30, April 21, and May 6, 1925, were preserved among McGinnis's papers in the files of the *Southwest Review*, of which he was an editor. For photocopies and permission to quote from them, I am grateful to Allen Maxwell, Director of the Southern Methodist University Press.

4. Collins, *New Orleans Sketches*, p. 132. All subsequent quotations from the essay are from this edition.

5. Faulkner's contributions to the *Times-Picayune* are collected in *New Orleans Sketches*. Typescripts of several other stories written at about the same time, but unpublished, including "Peter" and "Don Giovanni," are in the Berg Collection of the New York Public Library. See Blotner, pp. 425, 446.

6. Faulkner, *Flags in the Dust* (New York: Random House, 1973), pp. 267-268; the passage appears on pp. 278–79 of *Sartoris* (New York: Harcourt, Brace, 1929) (the original publication of a truncated version of the novel).

7. Anderson himself used the story in a letter to Faulkner that was written during that same spring of 1925 and that was part of the Al Jackson tall-tale series the two men were working up together. Anderson's version concerned one Flu Balsam:

> This Flu, it seems, had been herding cows over in Texas, but had lost his horse. He was a nervous, erratic kind of a man with a

tin ear got from the kick of a horse, and if he had web feet, like they say so many of the fishherds get, I couldn't notice. He had on congress shoes.

About his losing his horse. It seems he couldn't sleep much nights, and so he traded his horse to an easygoing, restful kind of a Texan, and an expert sleeper, for a night's sleep. The fellow was to come around about seven in the evening to get the horse, and Flu was to get his sleep, and so Flu got the horse out in front of his house early and stood holding him, all ready to rush off to bed, but the fellow didn't show up till almost four in the morning.

*Letters of Sherwood Anderson,* ed. Howard Mumford Jones and Walter Rideout (Boston: Little, Brown, 1953), p. 163. See also Blotner, pp. 403–04.

8. Carbon copies of his letters of August 16 and November 21, 1927, were retained by Stone in his files. I am grateful to the late Mr. Stone for permitting me to quote them. They are now among the Stone papers in the Humanities Research Center, University of Texas.

9. Carvel Collins, "Faulkner and Anderson: Some Revisions," paper delivered at the meeting of the Modern Language Association, December 27, 1967, in New York; quoted by McHaney, p. 467.

10. The records of Harold Ober, Faulkner's agent, reveal that the piece was received on February 24, 1953, and sent on (after retyping) to the *Atlantic* the same day at the "author's request." A memorandum dated March 11, also in the Ober files, notes that the *Atlantic* has changed the "original plan slightly, and will now run the Faulkner piece independently, in the same issue, but having no connection with the letters." It was published, with the changed title "Sherwood Anderson: An Appreciation," *Atlantic,* 191 (June 1953), 27–29.

11. The considerable difference between the 1925 and 1953 versions of the telling of Anderson's horse/sleep dream might be taken as a measure of Faulkner's distinction between fact and truth, for example.

12. "A Note on Sherwood Anderson," in *Essays, Speeches & Public Letters by William Faulkner,* ed. James B. Meriwether (New York: Random House, 1966), pp. 3–4. Subsequent quotations from the essay are from this edition, which is based on Faulkner's original typescript in the Ober files.

13. "Carcassonne" was first published in Faulkner's collection of stories, *These 13* (New York: Cape and Smith, 1931), although it may

have been written several years earlier. Blotner (p. 502) speculates that it may date from as early as 1925–26, though I should be inclined to place it later.

14. Letter from Faulkner to Beck, July 6, 1941. Part of it was quoted by Beck in his "Faulkner: A Preface and a Letter," *Yale Review*, 52 (October 1962), 159; for a copy of the entire letter I am indebted to Professor Beck, and for permission to quote from it I am grateful to Mrs. Jill Faulkner Summers.

15. "Mississippi Hills" is reproduced from an early version dated October 17, 1924, as Plate V in *"Man Working," 1919-1962: William Faulkner*, compiled by Linton Massey (Charlottesville: University Press of Virginia, 1968). A revised and shortened version appeared as "My Epitaph" in *Contempo*, I, February 1, 1932; and it was further revised as the untitled last poem in Faulkner's *A Green Bough* (New York: Smith and Haas, 1933). "Verse Old and Nascent" was first published in the *Double Dealer*, 7 (April 1925) and is reprinted in Carvel Collins, ed., *William Faulkner: Early Prose and Poetry* (Boston: Little, Brown, 1962); see esp. p. 116.

16. To an audience at Nagano in 1955, Faulkner made an interesting distinction between fiction and poetry that illustrates the significance of his decision to remain home, as a novelist, instead of becoming an exile from it, like most American writers:

> the poet deals with something which is so pure and so esoteric that you cannot say he is English or Japanese—he deals in something that is universal. That's the distinction I make between the prose writer and the poet, the novelist and the poet—that the poet deals in something universal, while the novelist deals in his own traditions.

*Lion in the Garden*, ed. James B. Meriwether and Michael Millgate (New York: Random House, 1968), p. 96.

17. Sherwood Anderson, "They Come Bearing Gifts," *American Mercury*, 21 (October 1930); esp. 129–30.

18. *Essays, Speeches & Public Letters*, p. 119.

19. *Faulkner in the University*, ed., Frederick L. Gwynn and Joseph L. Blotner (New York: Vintage, 1965), p. 20.

# Index